Prayers and Litanies for the Civic Year

by
LeRoy Koopman

Liturgical Publications
2875 South James Drive
New Berlin, WI   53151

ISBN 0-940169-11-8

Printed in the United States of America

ii

TABLE OF CONTENTS

CALLS TO WORSHIP

Leader: Choose this day whom you will serve and worship. Will you follow after the false gods of the land or will you worship and serve Yahweh, the one true God?

People: FAR BE IT FROM US THAT WE WOULD FORSAKE THE LORD TO SERVE OTHER GODS, FOR IT IS YAHWEH WHO HAS DELIVERED US FROM BONDAGE AND HAS DONE GREAT THINGS IN OUR SIGHT.

                                — Adapted from Joshua 24:15-17

Leader: Consider the days of old.

People: REMEMBER THE YEARS GONE BY

Leader: Will the Lord spurn forever,

People: AND NEVER AGAIN BE FAVORABLE?

Leader: Has his steadfast love forever ceased?

People: ARE HIS PROMISES AT AN END FOR ALL TIME?

Leader: Our God works wonders

People: AND HAS DEMONSTRATED HIS MIGHT AMONG THE PEOPLES.

Leader: With his arm God redeems his own

People: AND HE LEADS HIS PEOPLE LIKE A FLOCK.

                                  — Adapted from Psalm 77

The Lord has been our dwelling place in all generations. Before the mountains were brought forth, and before he formed the earth and all the universe, even from everlasting to everlasting, he has been God.

                                — Adapted from Psalm 90:1-2

Seek the Lord and his strength,
see his presence continually!
Remember the wonderful works that he has done,
his miracles, and the judgments he uttered.
He is mindful of his covenant forever,
of the word that he commanded
for a thousand generations.

                                — Psalm 105: 4-5, 8

Leader: Blessed be the name of God forever and ever,
          to whom belongs wisdom and might.
People: GOD CHANGES TIMES AND SEASONS:
          HE REMOVES RULERS AND SETS UP RULERS.
Leader: God gives wisdom to the wise
          and knowledge to those who have understanding.
People: GOD REVEALS DEEP AND MYSTERIOUS THINGS,
          KNOWING WHAT IS IN THE DARKNESS,
          AND THE LIGHT DWELLS WITH HIM.
Leader: To God, the God of our fathers,
          we will give thanks and praise.
                              —Adapted from Daniel 2:20-23a

On this first day of the new year,
It is fitting that we are found in the house of the Lord.
For it is from him that we have come.
It is in him that we live and move and have our being.
And it is he who gives eternal life.

This is a time of new beginnings:
the beginning of a new day;
the beginning of a new week;
the beginning of a new month;
the beginning of a new year.
Let us leave behind our yesterdays,
with their painful memories,
their bad decisions,
and the deliberate wanderings;
and let us turn our eyes
to the opportunities before us
and to the God who will lead us.

On this, the beginning of a new day
and the beginning of a new year,
Let us come before the Lord
        to catch a new vision
        to make a new commitment,
        and to declare a new love.

God is the Alpha and the Omega,
    the beginning and the end.
In Him the past and future converge
    into an eternal now.
Let us come before Him
    in our finitude
and seek from Him
    the secret of eternal life.

The God of Abraham, Isaac, and Jacob;
the God of Moses, Isaiah, and Amos;
the God of John, Peter, and Paul;
the God of (leaders of your religious heritage);
the God of (members of your congregation);
the God of every age and every continent;
the God of every tongue and tribe on the face of the earth
is *our* God in this year of our Lord, (current year).
Come, let us worship.

The Lord our God
is the Alpha and the Omega,
the beginning and the end,
our Creator and our Savior,
our Source and our Hope.
Therefore we come to pray and to praise,
to thank and to hope,
for the Lord our God is the eternal God.

INVOCATIONS

Leader: Lord, you have been our dwelling place in all generations.

People: BEFORE THE MOUNTAINS WERE BROUGHT FORTH, OR EVER YOU HAD FORMED THE EARTH AND THE WORLD,

Leader: From everlasting to everlasting you are God.

People: FOR A THOUSAND YEARS IN YOUR SIGHT ARE LIKE YESTERDAY WHEN IT IS PAST, OR AS A WATCH IN THE NIGHT.

Leader: So teach us to count our days that we may gain a wise heart.

People: SATISFY US IN THE MORNING WITH YOUR STEADFAST LOVE, SO THAT WE MAY REJOICE AND BE GLAD ALL OUR DAYS.

— Psalm 90: 1, 2, 4, 12, 14

At this date when we again mark the passage of time, we are deeply aware of our limitations, for our past is quickly forgotten and our future hides behind a veil.

Now as we worship, we do not ask that You will reveal to us some prophetic disclosure of what is to come, but rather that You will give us faith and courage to walk undaunted into the grey unknown.

It is fitting, O God of the ages, that we should bring this year to a conclusion in your special presence. You have brought us through joys and sorrows, laughter and tears, prosperity and poverty, health and sickness. Through it all you are still our God and we are still your people. Consecrate this hour as one of special thanks for the past and one of heartfelt commitment for the future.

You who are God of the ages,
the Alpha and Omega,
in whose sight a thousand years is as a day,
and in whom there is no shadow of turning;
become for us a rock of safety amid the raging torrent,
a citadel of truth on the shifting sands of time.

4

O God of the ages,
source of all creation and sustainer of all life,
we set aside this hour as a time of wonder,
in which we reflect on the mystery of life.
We set aside this hour as a time of thanksgiving,
as we consider the good things of the past year.
We set aside this hour as a time of worship,
as we honor you as the God of love and majesty.
We set aside this hour as a time of dedication
as we renew our commitment to the healing of your world.

Almighty God,
source and sustainer of all life,
who in your mercy has spared us
to see a new day and a new year,
may we begin this year with your favor,
continue it with your power,
and conclude it with your benediction.

We thank you, God, for memory which enables us — when we look to the future — to build on the past.

We thank you, God, for imagination which enables us — when we build for the future — to transcend the past.

We thank you, God, for the power of will which enables us to bring memory and imagination together in an active *now.*

May the present moment be for us a time of wonder, a time of worship, a time of thanks, and a time of reflection as we enter a new year.

You, O God, are the beginning and the end.
    You are our creator, savior, and sustainer.
From you we have come, and to you we shall return.
    In you we live and move and have our being.
Therefore it is right that we should come to you
    on this dawn of the new year
and publicly proclaim our faith, our worship, and our love,
    in this life and the life to come.

As the glory of the Lord
enveloped the shepherds at the birth of Christ,
so may that glory surround us today,
comforting us with your presence,
filling us with a sense of awe,
and inspiring us to begin this new year
with enthusiasm and confidence.

O Lord our God, grant us grace to desire you with our whole heart;
so that so desiring, we may seek and find you; and so finding you
we may love you; and loving you we may hate those sins from
which you have redeemed us; for the sake of Jesus Christ.

—Anselm, 1033-1109

O merciful Father,
we are grateful for your providence in the year past.
We seen evidence of your presence in our lives.
You have clothed, fed, and preserved us,
and even in our sorrows you have been there
to encourage us to go on.
So on this first day of the new year
we worship you as the source of all good things
and open our lives to your Spirit for the year ahead.

PRAYERS OF CONFESSION

PRAYER OF CONFESSION

We confess, Lord, that we are afraid of the unknown and that we are prone to doubt in time of trouble.

When the storm clouds gather, we forget that there is a sun above.

We are bold to walk across green pastures and beside still waters, but we are apprehensive at the entrance to the valley of deep darkness.

We are grateful for the rain, but we begrudge the storm clouds which must accompany it.

Take away our human fears, Lord; our worry about many things; our sense of inadequacy about the present; and our apprehension over the future. Give us, O Holy Father, greater faith and a more steadfast hope. Forgive our failure to fully trust, and enable us to walk forward with a sure step and an uplifted face.

WORDS OF ASSURANCE

In the midst of uncertainty and flux, we can come to God,
   for his truth never changes,
   his power never wanes,
   his promises never fail,
   and his love never fades.

PRAYER OF CONFESSION

We confess, Lord, that we anguish over our yesterdays, we are dissatisfied with our todays, and we fret over our tomorrows.

We relive the grievances of the past, we complain about the inconveniences of the present, and we anticipate the dangers of the future.

Deliver us, O God, from an attitude which makes dissatisfaction a way of life.

Cleanse us, O holy Father, from a morbid preoccupation with trouble, for it poisons our souls.

Deliver us, O Lord, from the negativism which paralyzes our wills.

Grant us, O Holy Spirit, quiet confidence in your providence. Calm the restlessness in our souls, and overcome our discontent with the balm of your peace.

WORDS OF ASSURANCE

Since God has removed the wrongs of our past and has made our record clean, let us take heart, greeting the future with a new confidence and revived enthusiasm.

PRAYER OF CONFESSION

In your mercy, O God,
forgive what we have been in the past,
help us to correct what we are now,
and direct us in what we shall become in the future,
so that we may walk all our days in your ways
and may become all that we were meant to be.

WORDS OF ASSURANCE

We embrace and celebrate the promise of the apostle: "And you he
made alive, when you were dead through the trespasses and sins
in which you once walked."

— Ephesians 2:1-2

PRAYER OF CONFESSION

If we are living only in the past, idolizing the former days,
wringing our hands over the present, fearing the future,
FATHER, FORGIVE US.
If we are living only in the future, creating a dream world,
rejecting all tradition, avoiding the work before us,
FATHER, FORGIVE US.
If we are living only in the present, pursuing the pleasure of the
moment, ignoring heritage, making no plans for tomorrow,
FATHER, FORGIVE US.
Grant us, Father, the insight to see life whole, submitting it to
the Lordship of him who is the Alpha and Omega, the beginning
and the end.

WORDS OF ASSURANCE

In this find peace:
that our God is the same yesterday, today, and forever.
His promises never fail,
and his compassion never falters.

9

PRAYER OF CONFESSION

Leader: O God, who has been our help in ages past,
People: FORGIVE US IF WE HAVE NEGLECTED TO GIVE THANKS.
Leader: O God, who is our hope for years to come,
People: RESTORE US IF WE HAVE LIVED ANXIOUSLY.
Leader: O God, who is our guide while life shall last,
People: FORGIVE US IF WE HAVE INSISTED ON OUR OWN WAY.
Leader: O God, who is our eternal home,
People: PARDON US IF WE HAVE INVESTED IN THIS LIFE ONLY.

WORDS OF ASSURANCE

Leader: Under the shadow of his throne,
we still will dwell secure.
People: SUFFICIENT IS HIS ARM ALONE,
AND OUR DEFENSE IS SURE.
(Prayer of Confession and Words of Assurance adapted from "O God, Our Help in Ages Past," by Isaac Watts)

PRAYER OF CONFESSION

O God of holiness and truth,
who always keeps covenant with your people,
whose love is eternal,
and whose faithfulness is to all generations,
forgive us for the shallowness of our faith,
the temporary nature of our enthusiasm,
and the lack of intensity in our commitment.
Restore to us the joy of our salvation
and incline us this year, by your Word and Spirit,
to be your holy and loyal people.

WORDS OF ASSURANCE

Hear the good news! This Jesus whom you follow is the Alpha and the Omega, the beginning and the end; the one who forgives the past and gives hope for the future.
10

PRAYER OF CONFESSION

God of light and power and love,
  We confess that we hesitate at the brink of the future.
Seeing light at the end of the dark passageway,
  we yet loiter in the darkness.
Even with Christ walking in love beside us,
  we dread the unknown foe.
Although you have promised to be our refuge and strength,
  we are uncertain and afraid.
Dispel our fears, we pray,
  and evaporate the shadows with your holy light.

WORDS OF ASSURANCE

We can be sure that neither things present nor things to come will
be able to separate us from the love of God in Christ Jesus our
Lord.

— Adapted from Romans 8:39

PRAYER OF CONFESSION

Too often, Lord, we are shackled by the past,
and our yesterdays have made our todays a nightmare.
We are poisoned by the bitterness of ancient wrongs.
We are carrying the load of sins long forgiven.
We are obsessed with what might have been.
Save us, Lord, from the tyranny of history,
teach us to believe in the cleansing power of new beginnings,
and set us free to serve you with freedom and joy.

WORDS OF ASSURANCE

Our God is a God of new beginnings,
a God who removes our sins as far as the east is from the west,
a God of second chances and new opportunities,
a God who is not willing that any should perish,
a God who sends us on our way with a song in our hearts.

PRAYER OF CONFESSION

Leader: For looking behind with regret,
People: FORGIVE US AND GIVE US PEACE.
Leader: For looking around us with greed,
People: FORGIVE US AND GIVE US CONTENTMENT.
Leader: For looking ahead with fearfulness,
People: FORGIVE US AND GIVE US A SENSE OF
ADVENTURE.
Leader: For looking upward with doubt,
People: FORGIVE US AND GIVE US FAITH.

WORDS OF ASSURANCE

Trust in the Lord,
for he will bind your wounds,
calm your nerves,
ease your pain,
restore your confidence,
and forgive your sins.

PRAYER OF CONFESSION
AND
WORDS OF ASSURANCE

Leader: We confess that we have not fully experienced the new life, nor are we already perfect,
People: BUT WE PRESS ON TO MAKE THAT GOAL OUR OWN, BECAUSE JESUS CHRIST HAS MADE US HIS OWN.
Leader: Forgetting that which lies behind, and straining forward to what lies ahead,
People: WE PRESS ON TOWARD THE GOAL FOR THE PRIZE OF THE UPWARD CALL OF GOD IN CHRIST JESUS.
Leader: For our commonwealth is in heaven, and from it we await a Savior, the Lord Jesus Christ,
People: WHO WILL CHANGE OUR LOWLY BODIES TO BE LIKE HIS GLORIOUS BODY, BY THE POWER WHICH ENABLES HIM TO BRING EVERYTHING UNDER HIS CONTROL.

—Adapted from Philippians 3:12-16, 20-21

GENERAL PRAYERS

PRAYER OF THANKSGIVING
(For the year just past)

As we stand at the doorway of the new year, we pause to give thanks.

When we look back upon the roads we have traveled, we recall the valleys of dark shadows, the bright meadows of delight, the cool shade of relaxation, the mountaintops of ecstacy. For these we give thanks.

We remember the busy streets, the shopping centers, the dangerous alleys, the noisy factories, the quiet offices. For these we give thanks.

We have walked lonely roads, we have rubbed shoulders on crowded sidewalks, we have driven on busy highways, we have glided through the skies. For these we give thanks.

We remember the banter of the kitchen, the relaxation of the family room, the fun of the back yard, the love of the bedroom, the provisions of the dining room. For these we give thanks.

We have shivered in the cold, we have sweltered in the sun, we have marveled at the sunsets, we have been lifted in spirit by the brightness of the day, and we have found peace in the dark of the night. For these we give thanks.

PRAYER OF PRAISE AND PETITION
(For the year just past)

As we look back across the year, we remember the many events which have molded our lives. We name them before you, some with praise, some with confession, some with sorrow, and others with celebration. Each event has left a need, or a challenge, or a blessing, and we bring these before you as petitions. Naming our own personal details, we bring before you —
- — family events which were especially meaningful (pause)
- — personal events which changed us (pause)
- — events in the life of our church (pause)
- — events in the life of our community (pause)
- — events in the life of our nation (pause)
- — events in the life of our world (pause)

13

PRAYER OF THANKSGIVING
(For new beginnings)

At the beginning of a new day, a new week, a new month, and a new year, we raise our prayer of thanks for the opportunity of new beginnings.

We thank you for new beginnings in periods of time. We see in our clocks and calendars a reflection of the orderliness of your creation, a fulfillment of the biblical statement that for everything there is a season.

We thank you for new beginnings in the dynamics of our lives. We are grateful for the celebration of birthdays, anniversaries, and other special days which give us an opportunity to celebrate together the goodness of our existence and the warmth of our lives together.

We are grateful also for new beginnings in the sense of second opportunities and fresh starts. We are thankful that failure need not be final, that sins can be forgiven, that mistakes can be remedied. Help us, God, never to give up, never to say that the cause is hopeless, never to say that the situation is beyond hope.

PRAYER OF PETITION
(For perspective)

O God of the ages, at the beginning of a new year we ask for a proper perspective on the year now ended.

Where we have succeeded, help us to give credit to those who have contributed to our success, and help us to verbalize our gratitude. Where we have failed, encourage us regarding the future and keep us from brooding over the past.

Where we have sinned, help us to be honestly repentant and grant us the assurance of our pardon. Where we have alienated others, give us the grace to be kind and patient, peacemakers in our circle of friends and family.

Where life has been cruel, keep us from bitterness and despair, and open our eyes to the promise of the future. Where life has been good, help us to enjoy and savor it, counting each moment precious and celebrating the life you have given.

PRAYER OF PETITION
(For the year ahead)

We pray for clear thinking in the year ahead. May we rely on your Word for direction instead of trusting in our own unreliable impulses, in silly advice from astrologers, and in insignificant happenstances of life.

May we be conscious of the subtle pressure of our society to conform to its twisted standards, and may we have the courage of our convictions to stand strong against what we know is wrong.

May we be instruments of constructive change, alert to the injustices and inequities of our society. Give us the courage to act, the wisdom to take steps that are appropriate, and the patience to follow through despite setbacks.

PRAYER OF THANKSGIVING
(For the blessings of the past year)

Hear our prayer of thanksgiving for the blessings, opportunities, and challenges of the year just past.

We give thanks for old acquaintances we have met, for new friends we have made, for the luxuries we have enjoyed, for the places we have visited, and for the new insights we have gained.

We are grateful for help and comfort through the painful and difficult times — the serious illness, the family problems, the death of a loved one, the financial crisis.

We are thankful for the special events which we have celebrated within our family circles: the engagements, the weddings, the birthdays, the anniversaries, the new jobs, the graduations, the birth of children, and many other events of personal and family importance.

In retrospect, we can even be thankful for some of the difficulties we encountered and the disappointments we endured. Even though unpleasant, they were learning experiences for us, and through them our characters were strengthened and our resolve was made strong.

We give thanks for prayers that have been answered, for the spiritual growth we have experienced, for the sense of your presence we have enjoyed. And, most of all, we are grateful for Jesus Christ, in whose name we pray.

COVENANT FOR THE NEW YEAR

Leader: As we begin a new year, let us renew our covenant with God and with each other.

People: WE WILL MAKE SOLEMN VOWS TO LOVE GOD WITH HEART, SOUL, AND MIND, AND TO LOVE OUR NEIGHBORS AS OURSELVES.

Leader: How will you love the Lord your God?

People: WE WILL BE FAITHFUL IN WORSHIP; WE WILL HONOR GOD'S NAME; WE WILL WALK IN THE WAYS GOD HAS REVEALED; AND WE WILL PROCLAIM IN WORD AND DEED GOD'S GOOD NEWS OF SALVATION.

Leader: And how will you love your neighbor as yourselves?

People: WE WILL BE KIND AND CONSIDERATE TOWARD ALL THOSE WHO ARE AROUND US; WE WILL ADVOCATE JUSTICE FOR THE OPPRESSED; WE WILL SEEK RELIEF FOR THE POOR; WE WILL WORK FOR PEACE IN OUR TIME; WE WILL BE HONEST AND TRUTHFUL IN ALL OUR DEALINGS; WE WILL BE FAITHFUL TO OUR SOLEMN VOWS; AND WE WILL EVEN TRY TO LOVE OUR ENEMIES.

Leader: Will you accomplish all this by yourselves?

People: NO, WE WILL RELY ON THE HOLY SPIRIT TO GIVE US POWER; WE WILL LOOK TO JESUS AS OUR EXAMPLE; AND WE WILL SEEK THE NURTURE AND SUPPORT OF THE CHURCH.

WORDS OF ENCOURAGEMENT

Leader: Will you be successful in this solemn covenant?

People: NOT ENTIRELY, BUT WE WILL NOT THEREBY BECOME DISCOURAGED, BECAUSE WE CAN SAY WITH THE APOSTLE JOHN, "TO ALL WHO RECEIVED HIM, WHO BELIEVED IN HIS NAME, HE GAVE POWER TO BECOME CHILDREN OF GOD."

— John 1:12

OFFERTORY SENTENCES

As we begin the new year, it is well to review once again the words of our Savior: "Strive first for the kingdom of God and his righteousness, and all these things will be given to you as well."
— Matthew 6:33

"Everyone who hears these words of mine and does them," said Jesus, "will be like a wise person who built a house upon a rock." Let us, in our giving, hear the words of Jesus and do them.
— Adapted from Matthew 7:24

Godliness with contentment is great gain. For we brought nothing into the world, and we can take nothing out of it. But if we have food and clothing, we will be content with that.
— 1 Timothy 6:6-8, NIV

Let this offering be symbolic of the complete commitment of time, talents, and energy that we make to God — for the extension of God's kingdom and for the welfare of all humankind.

On this, the first (day) (Sunday) of the new year, let us make a new commitment to Jesus Christ and to the good news he came to bring.

It is fitting that we begin this year, not only by receiving but also by giving. In so doing we make for ourselves a declaration of priorities and we state before the congregation and the world that Jesus Christ is first in our lives.

Some things we invest in will last a few days,
others a few months,
still others a few years,
and a very few things will last a lifetime.
But only those things which we invest in God and his kingdom will
    last forever.

OFFERTORY PRAYERS

On this, the first day of the year, we commit ourselves to Jesus Christ and pledge to build our lives upon his words. Receive these gifts as proof of our commitment and obedience.

So often, Lord, our values become tangled. In our urgency to gain the present advantage, we lose sight of the long-range goal. Grant to us this year, in all of our stewardship of life and money, the gift of wisdom and the spirit of commitment.

Thank you, Father, for the things you have entrusted to us —
food and clothing, homes and money,
talents of mind and body,
hours, and days, and years.
May we realize that these things are not ends in themselves,
but are part of our total responsibility
to ourselves, to our God, and to our world.

We thank you, God of the ages, for this opportunity of investing in eternity; for your people will forever live and your kingdom will never come to an end.

On this, the first day of the new year, we express our priorities by sharing these gifts. Help us always to put first things first and to gain a proper perspective on the meaning of our possessions.

We are grateful, Father, for this opportunity of being participants in the eternal, for through these gifts our compassion is invested in a cause that will never fail and in souls that will never die.

In you, O Lord, we live and move and have our being. Teach us that none of what we are, or have, is truly our own, but is a divine and holy trust. Every moment is sacred, as is every possession and every gift. Consecrate, then, not just these few dollars, but all that we are and have, to your glory.

We give thanks, Lord, that we can take these transitory, worldly possessions and give them eternal significance by investing them in the truths which never age, and in the souls which never die.

We are grateful, God of the ages, for the satisfaction of knowing that when we invest in your kingdom we are investing in eternity. Receive, with our thanks, these immortal offerings.

Leader: Because you hold first place in our lives,
People: RECEIVE WITH OUR VOWS OF LOYALTY THESE OFFERINGS.
Leader: Because we wish to begin the new year with an act of commitment,
People: RECEIVE WITH OUR DEDICATION THESE OFFERINGS.
Leader: Because we are grateful for what you have done for us in the past and anticipate with faith what you will do with us in the future,
People: RECEIVE WITH OUR THANKS THESE OFFERINGS.

It's the first Sunday of the year, and a good time for us to set priorities. We give these gifts with love and with prayer, indicating that the cause of Christ is uppermost in our minds and dear to our hearts.

BENEDICTIONS

The Lord is your keeper;
    the Lord is your shade on your right hand.
The Lord will keep you from all evil;
    he will keep your life.
The Lord will keep your going out and your coming in,
    from this time forth and forever more.

— Psalm 121:5, 7, 8

When you come to the end of life's journey, may you be able to say with the aged Simeon after he saw the child Jesus in the Temple: "Lord, now let your servant depart in peace, for my eyes have seen your salvation."

— Adapted from Luke 2:29-30

Run with patience the race that is set before you,
forgetting the things that are behind,
straining forward to reach the things that are ahead,
and, finally, by God's mercy,
obtaining the crown of life.

— Inspired by Philippians 3:12-16

You are surrounded by a great cloud of witnesses, so lay aside anything that would slow your progress and the sins that are a heavy weight, and run with enthusiasm the race that is set before you. Keep your eyes upon Jesus, who has run the race before you and is cheering you on.

— Adapted from Hebrews 12:1-2

May the God of Abraham, Isaac, and Jacob,
the God of Peter, James, and John,
The God of all who have called upon him
in all the ages of the world,
bless you and keep you always
in the name of his Son, Jesus Christ.

May God grant you joy in loving,
certainty in believing,
and fulfillment in serving,
now and until the end of your lives.

During the year which is ahead,
may the warmth of God's love be your comfort;
may the light of God's wisdom be your guide;
and may the certainty of God's promises be your confidence.

Throughout this new year
may you experience
fulfillment in your labor,
delight in your love,
sympathy in your grief,
healing in your illness,
mutuality in your happiness,
and excitement in your faith.

When life's shadows lengthen;
when the heat of the day
gives way to the coolness of the evening;
when God calls you home
and your work is done;
may you be found faithful to your Savior,
still walking with him and his people.

Learn from yesterday.
Live for today.
Hope for tomorrow.

Go forward in faith,
being confident that in the end
good will triumph over evil,
light will dispel darkness,
truth will expose error,
and life will triumph over death.

The Lord who in mercy forgives the past
and in hope sends us into the future
now grants us the assurance of his abiding presence.

CALLS TO WORSHIP

Leader: We shall greatly rejoice in the Lord;
People: OUR SOULS SHALL EXULT IN OUR GOD.
Leader: For he has clothed us with the garments of salvation,
People: AND HAS COVERED US WITH THE ROBES OF RIGHTEOUSNESS,
Leader: As a bridegroom decks himself with a garland,
People: AND AS A BRIDE ADORNS HERSELF WITH JEWELS.
— Adapted from Isaiah 61:10

As we gather to worship
we say with Mary, the mother of Jesus,
our souls magnify the Lord,
and our spirits rejoice in God our Savior.
— Adapted from Luke 1:46b-47

As a shepherd seeks a sheep who has wandered,
as a father and mother seek a lost child,
so the Lord God seeks his own.
Come, let us honor the God who seeks.

As the boy Jesus, at the age of 12,
lingered in the Temple,
asking and answering life's great questions,
so we, in these latter days,
must also be about our Father's business,
learning from each other and from the Word,
preparing ourselves for ministry.

Said the writer of early America, Washington Irving: "The dullest observer must be sensible of the ardor and serenity prevalent in those households where the occasional exercise of a beautiful form of worship in the morning gives, as it were, the keynote to every temper for the day, and attunes every spirit to harmony." Believing this to be true, let us worship the Lord our God.

Come, let us worship and honor,
let us sit at the feet of the Savior.
We will learn the wisdom of the Lord,
and we will share his truth and his compassion.

When our glamour fades,
when our pleasures bore us,
and when our money buys emptiness,
the presence of the Lord
is like a bubbling spring in the desert,
and like welcoming arms at the end of the day.

God has given us life.
God has given us the good earth.
God has given us people to love.
God has given us Jesus Christ.
What more can we ask?
Come, let us worship the Lord our God.

Come, let us worship the God
whose love is like that of a mother for her child,
whose arms are ever reaching out,
whose eyes are always alert,
and whose hands are ever compassionate.

INVOCATIONS

We praise you this morning as the God of life, the God of home, the God of peace, the God of love, the God of hope. As we gather for worship, we ask you to truly become the God of our lives and the God of our homes. Become the source of our peace, our love, and our hope, in the name of your Son.

For the dawning of a new day,
for the comfort of this house of worship,
for the companionship of fellow Christians,
for the loving circle of our families,
and for the presence of the Holy Spirit,
we raise our prayer of thanks.

Restore, O Lord, our sense of the presence of the divine. Amid the rush of traffic and the confusion of many voices, may we hear in our inner heart your word of encouragement and peace. Amid the shrill voices and explosive anger of our troubled world, may we sense your stabilizing presence. Amid the painful experience of family tensions and of our relationships gone awry, may we follow the pattern of your sacrificial love.

Help us, Lord, to slow down,
to take time for restoration,
to relax from our busyness,
to replenish our bodies and souls,
to learn from you,
to absorb your love,
and to go from this place refreshed.

We have drunk deeply of our beverages,
  and we are still thirsty.
We have gorged ourselves at our tables,
  but we are still hungry.
We have experienced the pleasures of body and mind,
  but are still unsatisfied.
So we stand beside the tree of life,
and beside the river of the water of life,
eager for the nourishment which satisfies our souls.

We have come, O God, to celebrate the power of love:
the love we know in our families,
the love we experience in our church,
the love we enjoy among friends
and even among complete strangers.
We praise you for this love,
for we know that all of it has its source in your great heart
and that it reached its fullest expression
in Jesus Christ our Lord.

As Mary and Joseph took the boy Jesus with them to the Temple at Jerusalem, so we have gathered our families to worship in this place.

We come to you as a covenant God, claiming your solemn promises for all who are members of our households of faith.

O God,
who cannot be confined by the borders of the universe,
or encompassed by the limitations of time,
or reduced to the most complicated of mathematical formulas,
or comprehended by the most brilliant of minds,
we are grateful that we can sing with little children,
"Jesus loves me, this I know, for the Bible tells me so."

O Father in heaven,
who cares for us as your children,
grant that we, like the Christ child,
may increase in maturity,
growing in favor with you
and with all those around us.

We are grateful, Lord God,
for the day you have given us,
for the call to faith you have extended,
for the freedom with which we can gather,
for our friends and family who are with us,
and for our faithful Savior, Jesus Christ,
who is our reason for being here.

We gather today as families —
as human families,
as the children of the most high God,
as brothers and sisters of our Lord Jesus Christ.
Help us, Lord, to gather together in harmony and in peace,
drawn together by the love which has its origin in heaven,
and is lived out on earth.

Family

PRAYERS OF CONFESSION
AND
WORDS OF ASSURANCE

PRAYER OF CONFESSION

Leader: For sins which we have committed as members of our personal families and as members of the family of God,

People: FORGIVE US, O GOD.

Leader: For thoughts which were bitter, or jealous, or lustful,

People: FORGIVE US, O HOLY SPIRIT.

Leader: For words which were angry, or cruel, or untrue,

People: FORGIVE US, O CHRIST.

Leader: For actions which were selfish, or hurtful, or dishonest.

People: FORGIVE US, O LORD.

Leader: For attitudes which were unloving, unforgiving or unsupportive,

People: FORGIVE US, O GOD.

WORDS OF ASSURANCE

Be assured of this,
that God was in Christ,
not only reconciling us to himself,
but also reconciling us to one another.

— Adapted from 2 Corinthians 5:19

PRAYER OF CONFESSION

We know, God, that you are the creator of the family,
the author of love, and the designer of marriage.
We acknowledge that we have fallen short of the standards you
  have established,
and that we have failed to achieve the joy and fulfillment which
  could be ours,
Forgive us, Lord, if in our closest relationships we have been
  selfish,
and if in our marriages we have not been fully committed.
Teach us, Lord, how to give and to receive love,
and help us to pattern our affection after the love which sacrifices
  and heals.

WORDS OF ASSURANCE

We have this confidence, that God's rules for living are meant for
our own happiness and welfare, and that when we truly receive
God's pardon we also receive power to transform our lives.

PRAYER OF CONFESSION

We come with feelings of guilt about the way we have treated those closest to us.

When we are out of sorts, we allow our bad humor to spread through our families like a dark fog.

In subtle ways we keep reminding our husbands, our wives, our children, and others about their faults.

When others have tried to talk to us about their pain and their concerns, we have kept the conversation centered on the superficial.

We have been jealous of relatives, of friends, and of neighbors, refusing to compliment them on their successes.

Intent on following our own pursuits, we have failed to spend the time we should with our families.

Forgive us where we have failed, and teach us to truly love.

WORDS OF ASSURANCE

The Lord is just in all his ways
and kind in all his doings.
The Lord is near to all who call upon him,
to all who call upon him in truth.

— Psalm 145:17-18

PRAYER OF CONFESSION

Leader: If we have sinned against our earthly father,
          if we have failed to appreciate his sacrifices,
          if we have not given him the honor he deserves,
People: FATHER IN HEAVEN, FORGIVE.
Leader: If we have been disobedient,
          if we have been disrespectful,
          if we have been critical,
People: FATHER IN HEAVEN, FORGIVE.
Leader: If we have failed to sympathize with his problems,
          if we have closed our ears to his advice,
          if we have dishonored his good name,
People: FATHER IN HEAVEN, FORGIVE.
Leader: If we have forgotten to express our thanks,
          if we have neglected to say, "I love you,"
          if we have failed to tell him we care,
People: FATHER IN HEAVEN, FORGIVE.

WORDS OF ASSURANCE

As a father has compassion on his children, so the Lord has
compassion on those who fear him.

— Psalm 103:13, NIV

PRAYER OF CONFESSION

Leader: If in our home life we have taken each other for granted.

People: FATHER, FORGIVE, AND RESTORE OUR LOVE.

Leader: If we have been insensitive to each other's hurts,

People: FATHER, FORGIVE, AND RESTORE OUR LOVE.

Leader: If we have been unwilling to listen — to *really* listen,

People: FATHER, FORGIVE, AND RESTORE OUR LOVE.

Leader: If we have been short-tempered and irritable,

People: FATHER, FORGIVE, AND RESTORE OUR LOVE.

Leader: If we have dragged up old hurts from the past,

People: FATHER, FORGIVE, AND RESTORE OUR LOVE.

Leader: If we have been unwilling to apologize,

People: FATHER, FORGIVE, AND RESTORE OUR LOVE.

Leader: If we have withheld the expression of our affection,

People: FATHER, FORGIVE, AND RESTORE OUR LOVE.

Leader: If we have allowed old animosities to simmer in our souls,

People: FATHER, FORGIVE, AND RESTORE OUR LOVE.

Leader: If we have failed to follow the example of Jesus' forgiving love,

People: FATHER, FORGIVE, AND RESTORE OUR LOVE.

WORDS OF ASSURANCE

Leader: While we were helpless, God gave us his very best.

People: WHILE WE WERE SINNERS, CHRIST DIED FOR US.

Leader: While we were his enemies, God made us his friends.

People: WE BELIEVE THESE TRUTHS, AND WE ARE AT PEACE.

— Adapted from Romans 5:6-11

PRAYER OF CONFESSION

Leader: For the times we have neglected our family obligations,
People: FORGIVE US, O GOD.
Leader: For the times we have been indifferent to the needs of others,
People: FORGIVE US, O GOD.
Leader: For the times we have spoken words which offended,
People: FORGIVE US, O GOD.
Leader: For the times we have failed to honor our parents,
People: FORGIVE US, O GOD.
Leader: For the times we have judged others on the basis of nationality, gender, or race,
People: FORGIVE US, O GOD.

WORDS OF ASSURANCE

As a mother comforts a child, so God comforts us who are his children, forgiving our waywardness and assuring us that we are still loved as members of the family.

PRAYER OF CONFESSION

Forgive us, Father in Heaven, if we have sinned against our fathers on earth. Grant pardon if we have disappointed them or if we have been disrespectful to them. Absolve us if we have in any way besmirched their reputation or their memory.

Enable us who are fathers, or who plan to become fathers, to more accurately reflect the image of you, our Father in heaven, so that those who learn from us will learn about you.

WORDS OF ASSURANCE

Let us receive our assurance of pardon and hope from our Lord's words in today's gospel lesson: "I am the living bread which came down from heaven; if anyone eats of this bread, he will live forever."

— John 6:51

PRAYER OF CONFESSION

Save us from all delusions, all unworthy purposes, all uncharitable thoughts. Fill us with a consuming desire to know the truth; and having learned it, to live it.

Help us now to be nobler in every purpose, to be unwavering in every temptation, to be loving in every relationship, and to be faithful in every commitment.

WORDS OF ASSURANCE

Ask, and it will be given you; seek, and you will find; knock, and it will be opened to you. For everyone who asks receives, and he who seeks finds, and to him who knocks it will be opened.

— Luke 11:9-10

PRAYER OF CONFESSION

We are sorry for our sins
because we have hurt those whom we love.
We have offended those who are at a distance from us.
We have injured our own reputations and self-respect.
But most of all we have sinned against you, our God.
Cleanse us from our faults and restore us in your sight,
then help us to apologize to others
and to mend the relationships we have broken or endangered.

WORDS OF ASSURANCE

But to all who believed him, who believed in his name, he gave
power to become the children of God.

— John 1:12

PRAYER OF CONFESSION

Leader: For anniversaries and birthdays forgotten,
People: GOD OF THE FAMILY, FORGIVE US.
Leader: For sacrifices which have gone unacknowledged,
People: FATHER OF OUR LORD JESUS CHRIST, FORGIVE
           US.
Leader: For appreciation which has never been verbalized,
People: GOD OF LOVE, FORGIVE US.
Leader: For the times we have caused bitter disappointment,
People: SEEKER OF THE PRODIGAL, FORGIVE US.
Leader: For the words spoken in unthinking harshness,
People: AUTHOR OF GENTLENESS, FORGIVE US.
Leader: For taking for granted our very existence,
People: CREATOR OF LIFE, FORGIVE US.

WORDS OF ASSURANCE

Like a mother, God comforts her children.
Like a father, God forgives and restores his own.

35

PRAYER OF CONFESSION

Leader: If we have offended anyone,
People: FATHER, FORGIVE, AND HELP US TO LOVE.
Leader: If we have disappointed our friends,
People: FATHER, FORGIVE, AND HELP US TO LOVE.
Leader: If we have worried our parents,
People: FATHER, FORGIVE, AND HELP US TO LOVE.
Leader: If we have neglected our spouse,
People: FATHER, FORGIVE, AND HELP US TO LOVE.
Leader: If we have been discourteous to strangers,
People: FATHER, FORGIVE, AND HELP US TO LOVE.
Leader: If we have injured in any way the body of Christ,
People: FATHER, FORGIVE, AND HELP US TO LOVE.

WORDS OF ASSURANCE

Even when we are at our worst,
  we know that God loves us.
Even when our faith is faltering,
  we know that God loves us.
Even when we have lost contact with the Almighty,
  we know that God loves us.

PRAYER OF CONFESSION

Forgive us, author of all human affection and creator of all human institutions, for not being the kind of family that we could become.

As parents, we have sometimes been too lenient and we have sometimes been too strict. We have faltered in our example. We have deprived our children of our presence and affection.

As children, we have burdened our parents with worry as we have strived for freedom and independence. We have failed in giving respect and affection. We have deprived them of some of the satisfactions of parenthood.

Heal our differences, we pray, and grant us that strong love which overcomes all difficulties, seeks a solution to all problems, and cuts across all barriers of age and generation.

WORDS OF ASSURANCE

We can ask God for the healing of our families because we, in turn, are part of his family. "When we cry, 'Abba! Father!' it is the Spirit himself bearing witness with our spirit that we are children of God, and if children, then heirs, heirs of God and fellow heirs with Christ."

— Romans 8:15-17a

PRAYER OF CONFESSION

We confess, Lord, that in our marriage relationships we do not always live up to the high ideals you have set for us.

We do not always subject ourselves to each other out of reverence for Christ. We do not always love each other as Christ loved the church. We do not always nourish and tenderly care for each other as Christ does for us. We do not always leave our old loyalties behind. We do not always display love and respect.

Help us, Lord of the church and Lord of the home, to pattern our love after yours.

— Inspired by Ephesians 5:21-33

WORDS OF ASSURANCE

Like a father, God has forgiven us.
Like a mother, God has quieted our fears.
Like a brother or sister, God has listened to our concerns.
Like a friend, God has encouraged us along the way.

PRAYER OF CONFESSION

We praise you for the institution of the family: for the closeness we experience, for the memories we share, for the encouragement and mutual support we receive, for the love which we both give and receive.

Nevertheless, we acknowledge that we have much to accomplish before we reach the ideal you have set before us. Some of us are angry. Some of us are hurt. Some of us are rebellious. Some of us are wandering. Some of us are without feeling. Some of us are indifferent.

Bind us together, Lord. Restore to us the joy and the closeness that we once knew. Enable us to experience that beautiful unity which is possible only when we live according to your plan.

WORDS OF ASSURANCE

The Almighty God, who is merciful as well as holy, loving as well as righteous, will pardon our sins, cleanse our inner being, fill us with love, and bring us to eternal life.

PRAYER OF CONFESSION

We who are children confess that we have not always kept your commandment to honor our fathers. We have not always demonstrated obedience where obedience is due, or given respect where respect is due, or expressed love where love is due.

We who are fathers confess that we have not always lived up to the ideals that you have set before us in your Word. We have not always demonstrated an example worthy to be followed, or given our families the time they deserved, or displayed the love and concern which are so desperately needed in these cold and difficult times.

Help us, as parents and children, to do our part in creating a family life which is loving, stable, and fulfilling, to our enrichment and to your glory.

WORDS OF ASSURANCE

Take heart, for within the family of God
there is forgiveness and restoration,
love and acceptance,
peace and promise.

PRAYER OF CONFESSION

Leader: For neglecting family devotions and prayer,
People: FATHER, FORGIVE US AND HEAL OUR HOMES.
Leader: For exchanging harsh words and dragging out old grievances,
People: FATHER, FORGIVE US AND HEAL OUR HOMES.
Leader: For failing to respect individuality and confidentiality,
People: FATHER, FORGIVE US AND HEAL OUR HOMES.
Leader: For expecting perfection of each other that belongs alone to you,
People: FATHER, FORGIVE US AND HEAL OUR HOMES.
Leader: For failing to honor and to cherish,
People: FATHER, FORGIVE US AND HEAL OUR HOMES.

WORDS OF ASSURANCE

The promises of God, said Peter, are "to you and to your children and to all that are far off, every one whom the Lord our God calls to him."

— Acts 2:39

PRAYER OF CONFESSION

Leader: If we as fathers have failed to give our families the time, the love, or the example they deserve,

People: FORGIVE US AND BIND US TOGETHER IN LOVE.

Leader: If we as wives have failed to give our husbands the understanding, the support, and the love they need,

People: FORGIVE US AND BIND US TOGETHER IN LOVE.

Leader: If we as young sons and daughters have failed to give our parents the obedience and love they should have,

People: FORGIVE US AND BIND US TOGETHER IN LOVE.

Leader: If we as older sons and daughters have failed to give our parents the respect and love they deserve,

People: FORGIVE US AND BIND US TOGETHER IN LOVE.

Leader: If we as members of the church have not done enough to encourage and to help,

People: FORGIVE US AND BIND US TOGETHER IN LOVE.

Leader: If we as members of society have neglected to establish structures which encourage the stability of the home,

People: FORGIVE US AND BIND US TOGETHER IN LOVE.

WORDS OF ASSURANCE

Receive this assurance: as members of God's family and as members of the human family, you are loved, you are forgiven, and you are restored.

PRAYER OF CONFESSION

While the Scripture calls upon us to honor our fathers, we confess that we sometimes do not.

As children, we may be disobedient and take for granted the work he does for our food, home, toys, and clothing.

As young people, we may consider him to be old fashioned, quaint, and irrelevant to our lives.

As wives, we may have little sympathy for the frustrations of his work and the pressures of his family responsibility.

As those having our own families, we may be ignoring his need to be included in our circle of love and concern.

Help us to give our earthly fathers the honor, the respect, and obedience, and the love they desire. And in so doing we will be learning to honor you, our Father in Heaven.

WORDS OF ASSURANCE

As a father comforts his children, so the Lord comforts those who seek him, who come to him for forgiveness and strength.

Family

GENERAL PRAYERS

PRAYER OF THANKS
(For the miracle of motherhood)

We thank you this morning for the special miracle we celebrate this day. We thank and praise you for the miracle of human life. We stand in awe of your plan to bring forth, from the love of two parents, a new life. We see a marvelous symbolism here, that the miracle of life and the miracle of love have been intertwined from the beginning of creation, both having their origin in you.

We praise you this morning for the miracle of a mother's love — a love which is patterned after the divine love; a love which never seems too tired to care; a love which persists even when spurned; a love which lifts up and comforts; a love which does not hesitate to discipline; a love which seeks the ultimate good above the immediate pleasure.

PRAYER OF INTERCESSION
(For mothers who have difficulties)

We raise our prayer of intercession for mothers who are experiencing difficulties in the task of raising children:
- for single mothers who have the task of being both father and mother to their children;
- for mothers who must deal with the strains of taking care of someone else's children in a second marriage;
- for mothers who would like to stay home with their children but who cannot because of financial necessity;
- for wives who would love to become mothers but who have not been able to have children;
- for mothers who must daily cope with the strains of a large family and its many demands;
- for mothers who grieve and are anxious because of the misconduct of their children.

PRAYER OF INTERCESSION
(For the rights of women)

O Lord God, who created both male and female in your own image and declared your handiwork to be good, we pray for the women of our world who are still struggling to be accepted as fully human.

We pray for those who are frustrated in the workplace because they are paid less than their male counterparts and find it impossible to advance beyond a certain level.

We pray for women of our world who are burdened with most of the work of the family and community, and those who have no choice except to bear an unmanageable number of children.

We pray for those women who must raise their children alone, those who are abused, and those who live in constant poverty.

We pray for those who are seldom given an opportunity to use their gifts, even in the church of Jesus Christ.

PRAYER OF INTERCESSION
(For mothers)

We pray today for those who celebrate Mothers' Day with mixed feelings:
— for those who desperately would like to become mothers, but who cannot;
— for those mothers whose lives have been shattered by the death of a child, who thus endure an agony almost unequaled in human experience;
— for those who have lost their mothers in death, who do not today have an opportunity to express their affection;
— for those who are stepmothers, stepdaughters, and stepsons; who must deal with a whole new set of dynamics and possible tensions in their relationships with each other;
— for those who are foster mothers, who are providing loving care for the unwanted, and who weep when a child they have come to love is taken away;
— for those who are hiding secret and painful hurts — of children sent away for adoption, and of decisions to move ahead with abortion.

45

PRAYER OF INTERCESSION
(For our homes)

On this day when we recognize the important role that our mothers play — or have played — in our lives, we raise a prayer of intercession for our homes.

We ask that our homes may be filled with love, that we may genuinely care for each other and be willing to sacrifice for each other.

We ask that our homes may be filled with patience, because in the course of everyday living we often have different opinions and we sometimes irritate each other.

We ask that our homes may be filled with friendship, that we may encourage each other to talk over the events of the day, to walk together, to spill out our worries and our concerns, and to share our successes and joys.

We ask that our homes may be characterized by faithfulness. May our bonds of loyalty be unbreakable, and may our absolute commitment to each other be assumed without a hint of wavering.

PRAYER OF THANKS AND INTERCESSION
(For our families)

We are thankful, O Lord, for our families — for those to whom we are bound not only by a blood relationship, but also by a relationship of affection, trust, and mutual support. We are grateful for their loyalty, their love, their trust, and their concern.

Strengthen the ties we have with one another. Give us patience when we are frustrated. Give us contentment when we see other people who have more than we have. Give us mutual trust when jealousy raises its head. Give us sympathy for the weaknesses and problems of those close to us. Give us a sense of humor when things don't go right. Help us to place the needs of others before our own. Give us, above all, an unswerving sense of commitment to each other, so that in good times and bad we will stand together.

PRAYER OF INTERCESSION
(For those who are lonely)

O God, who said at creation that it is not good for man to be alone, we pray this morning for those who are experiencing the emptiness of loneliness. We agonize for those who wish to have friends and to be a friend, but who cannot seem to make friends. Help them to determine the causes, and enable them to correct whatever is standing in the way.

Help us to break down the walls that separate us from each other, and give us the grace to reach out and welcome others. Make us sensitive to those who are shy and awkward, yet who crave the warmth of a smile and a spoken word. Help us to encourage, to praise, to touch the outstretched hand, to go the second mile, and to encourage one another in times of trouble.

We pray for those who, even within marriage, experience a sense of loneliness and estrangement; for those who for one reason or another have not been able to establish a satisfying and uplifting relationship. We pray that your self-giving love may become alive in their lives.

PRAYER OF INTERCESSION
(For special families)

On this day in which we celebrate the family and the role of motherhood, we are aware that many families include dynamics which are both a potential difficulty and a potential blessing.

We pray for single-parent families, recognizing that the mother or the father feels the responsibility of playing a dual role. Give these parents the mental, emotional, and physical stamina to carry on, often in the face of financial hardship.

We pray for blended families. Realizing that this can be a situation of trauma for children and of stress for parents, we pray for patience, wisdom, and a spirit of fairness.

We also pray for adoptive families, giving thanks for children who gladden the hearts; and giving thanks for warm and loving homes for those who otherwise would be deprived and lonely.

We pray for those couples who have a very empty place in their family circle, either because they are childless or because they have lost a child by death. The pain is very real, and we ask for the consolation of your Holy Spirit.

47

PRAYER OF INTERCESSION
(For families)

For families being destroyed by physical abuse, let us pray.
   (Pause)
For families being injured by verbal abuse, let us pray.
   (Pause)
For families being blended through remarriage, let us pray.
   (Pause)
For families who will be saying goodbye to a son or daughter, let us pray.
   (Pause)
For families being undermined by constant bickering, let us pray.
   (Pause)
For families facing financial difficulties, let us pray.
   (Pause)
For families threatened by infidelity, let us pray.
   (Pause)
For families who have suffered bereavement, let us pray.
   (Pause)
For families where there is stability and love, let us pray.
   (Pause)

PRAYER OF THANKS
(For fathers)

God of all things visible and invisible, whom we were encouraged by Jesus to address as "Our Father in Heaven," we raise our prayers of thanks and petition for our fathers on earth.

We thank you for their dedication to the task of making a living, for their love and devotion to their families, and for the example they have set for us. It is easy for us to be critical, so help us to recognize and acknowledge all that is good, helpful, comforting, and worthy of our imitation.

We pray that you will uphold the fathers of this congregation in the context of their offices, factories, and fields, and enable them to find satisfaction and fulfillment in all that they do.

PRAYER OF THANKSGIVING
(For our fathers)

We praise you, O Father in heaven, for the expression of yourself through fathers on earth; that despite all of the distortions caused by sin, your divine image in heaven is still reflected in the human image on earth.

We praise you, O Father, for life itself, and for your divine plan of giving us existence through the love of fathers and mothers.

We praise you, O Father, for your providence made concrete through our fathers on earth; for their long hours of work; for their sacrifices and skills; for their investment of time and talents on our behalf; for the food, clothing, and comfort we enjoy because of them.

We praise you, heavenly Father, for your love and concern for us as expressed through our earthly fathers; for their words of counsel and encouragement; for their affection; and for their willingness to help.

We praise you, heavenly Father, for your standards of life which are expressed through our earthly fathers; for their role models as family men and wage earners; and for their strong faith in times of testing.

PRAYER OF THANKS AND INTERCESSION
(For fathers)

We give thanks, our Father in Heaven, for our fathers on earth. We are grateful for the investments of time and energy they have made in our lives; for the long hours they have worked in our support; for the patience they have shown with our misdeeds; for the discipline they have exercised in our lives; for the love they have shared with us over the years; and for the legacy of faith they have left with us.

We pray for fathers who are going through difficult times: for those who are unemployed, for those who seem trapped in jobs they do not enjoy; for those who feel frustrated because they have not attained the goals they set for themselves; for those who are not able to spend much time with their families; for those who find it difficult to communicate their love for those closest to them.

We raise a prayer of petition for fathers who are in demanding circumstances. We pray for stepfathers who must deal patiently and wisely with complex family situations. We remember foster fathers, giving thanks for their dedication and praying that they may be equal to the task. We remember those who wish to become fathers, but who cannot. We pray for fathers who grieve the loss of a child by death, and for those who agonize over the waywardness of a son or daughter.

PRAYER OF PETITION
(For our home life)

Help us, Father, to become the kind of people who create homes which are loving, peaceful, productive, and godly.

May we be generous with our *time* — being willing to set aside our own hobbies and even our work to spend quality time with our loved ones. May we do so freely and ungrudgingly, setting a priority on those human relationships which really count.

May we be generous with our *empathy* — giving full attention to a son or daughter who is talking about a problem, or to a spouse who needs a listening ear. May we not simply nod absent-mindedly, but may we really try to understand.

May we be generous with our *love* — expressing fully what we feel in our hearts. May we find delight in our relationships with each other, and may we repeat over and over again our expressions of endearment. May there be no doubt in the minds of each of our family members that they are cherished, appreciated, and loved.

May we be generous with our *prayers* — bringing our deepest concerns and our happiest thanksgivings to your throne. May our family circle always include Jesus Christ, and may our family code always include the divine Word.

PRAYER OF THANKS
(For our families)

We give thanks, Father, for our families: for those who gather around the table at the evening meal; for those we can always count on when everyone else leaves; for those who know us well and love us anyway; for those who in turn depend on us for love and support; for brothers and sisters who are also best of friends; for children who give us so much pride and joy; for parents who provide a harbor of love and protection; and for those who despite our disagreements and irritations can forgive with a flourish.

PRAYER OF THANKSGIVING
(For the families of the church)

We raise our prayers of praise and thanks for all the families of our congregation.

We are thankful for prayers which are said, for Bible lessons that are read, for Christian principles that are taught.

We praise you for children who feel secure, for young people who love and respect their parents, and for parents who maintain a firm but even hand of discipline.

We are grateful for husbands and wives who are faithful despite all the pressures and opportunities to stray. We praise you for those who have determined to make their marriages work despite conditions which are far from ideal.

We are thankful for mothers and fathers who carry on valiantly even though they must do so without a partner present. We are grateful for those merged families who have overcome the tensions which could have torn them apart.

We are grateful for those single persons whose lives are fulfilled and successful, and for those who are willing to befriend the lonely and the bereaved.

OFFERTORY SENTENCES

Every day we make choices for ourselves and our families — choices about time, about priorities, about money. As we give, let us remember the words of the Old Testament hero Joshua: "Choose this day whom you will serve ... but as for me and my household, we will serve the Lord."

— Joshua 24:15

Having gifts that differ according to the grace given to us, let us use them — those who contribute, in liberality; those who give aid, with zeal; those who do acts of mercy, with cheerfulness.

— Adapted from Romans 12:6,8

Every generous act of giving, every perfect gift, is from above, coming down from the Father of lights.

— James 1:17a

The Apostle John said in his first letter, "Beloved, let us love one another, because love is from God; everyone who loves is born of God and knows God" (1 John 4:7). Let us now express this love through our tithes and offerings.

As the parents of Jesus brought sacrifices to the Temple, so we will bring these family offerings to this, our house of worship. May Christ's name be honored by our gifts, and may our families be strengthened as we share in sacrifice.

We give, not in order to win God's favor or to gain the admiration of others, but to express our thanks for all that you have done for us — for ourselves and for those we love.

As at Cana, Jesus took mere water and turned it into the wine of celebration and love, he will take these simple gifts and transform them into extraordinary expressions of mercy and grace.

As we give, we recognize the investment which other people have made in our lives. Our ancestors, our parents, our friends, and many others have all sacrificed to insure the blessings and freedoms we enjoy.

May the cycle not be broken. May those who follow us be able, like us, to look back in gratitude.

We give, not only as an end in itself, but also as an example to our children, our grandchildren, and all other members of our family. May they see in us an example of generosity and an attitude toward possessions which are worthy to be followed.

God's love inspires our love.
God's concern inspires our concern.
God's sacrifice inspires our sacrifice.

OFFERTORY PRAYERS

Leader: Because God has first loved us,
People: WE GIVE THESE OFFERINGS.
Leader: Because we are born of God and know God,
People: WE PRESENT THESE GIFTS.
Leader: Because we are now free to love others,
People: WE SHARE THESE RESOURCES.

In our family groupings we give to each other — because we love each other, honor each other, and seek each other's welfare. In our relationship to you we also give — because we love you, honor you, and seek the success of your worthy work on earth.

Some of us are without employment, and our gifts are less than they once were. Others of us are not only working but have received raises, so our gifts have increased in proportion. We know that you expect us to give according to what we have received, so we ask that you will accept with favor what we now present.

We present these gifts so people may continue to benefit from the ministry of this church:
    so couples may be united in marriage,
    so parents may bring their children for consecration,
    so inquirers may find answers to their questions,
    so the troubled may find an open ear,
    so the sick may be visited,
    so the Word may be proclaimed,
    and so your people may continue to worship in a place of holy beauty.

As we give, we realize that all of us on earth are members of one great family.

Enable us to truly care for each other, realizing that all of us are your children and created in your image.

We give these offerings because it has been our custom to do so at this particular place in the order of worship. In a sense, it is a ritual, and a good one. But we want it to be more than a ritual. We give these gifts as proof of a heart-felt commitment, as part of our total dedication to you and your cause.

As families — as brother, sister, parent, child, spouse — we help each other in times of need.

As your family — as brothers and sisters in Christ and as brothers and sisters in the family of mankind — we also express our mutual compassion. Accept these gifts as an expression of that concern and desire to help.

Receive, O God, these gifts — these offerings which not only advance the cause of Christ but leave a pattern for our families to follow, a pattern of devotion and sacrifice.

We present these offerings because we are concerned about our immediate families. For ourselves, our children, and our grandchildren, we desire a place and a program of Christian instruction and inspiration.

We also present these offerings because we are concerned about our church family around the world. Through these gifts we join hands with our brothers and sisters in Christ everywhere, celebrating our common faith.

We also present these offerings because we are concerned about the welfare of the whole family of mankind, created in your divine image. Through these offerings may the hungry be fed, the sick be healed, and the poor receive justice.

We have received a heritage of faith from those who have gone before us. It is our desire that we should leave a heritage of faith to our children and the generations yet to come. Bless these gifts, we pray, as they are invested in the lives of those who take up the flag of Christ after us.

Receive these gifts for what they are in themselves, but also for what they are as gifts from families — a mutual sharing, a mutual commitment, and a fine example for the children who will one day carry on the task.

BENEDICTIONS

You are leaving this temple of God,
but remember that you yourselves are living temples,
for the Spirit of God is alive within you.
                          — Adapted from 1 Corinthians 3:16

Whatever is true, whatever is noble, whatever is right, whatever is
pure, whatever is lovely, whatever is admirable — if anything is
excellent or praiseworthy — think about such things.
                          — Philippians 4:8, NIV

Receive the blessing of God Almighty:
the grace of life renewed,
the joy of life together,
and the promise of life to come,
through Jesus Christ our Lord.

May you so live
that you will bring help to others,
happiness to those who love you,
credit to yourself,
and honor to your Lord.

May God hold you in the hollow of his hand,
direct you by the instruction of his Word,
encourage you by the inspiration of his Spirit,
enfold you in the love of the family he has given you,
and sustain you by the companionship of his people.

May the hand of God protect you,
the power of God strengthen you,
and the wisdom of God instruct you
this day and all your days on earth.

May he who has prepared for you a house not made with hands,
eternal in the heavens, go with you now to your homes on earth;
and may you live together in harmony and holiness.

May God grant you joy in loving,
certainty in believing,
and fulfillment in serving,
now and until the end of your lives.

May faith energize you,
hope inspire you,
and love sustain you,
now and forever more.

May you be enriched by the love of your family and friends,
by the beauty of your world,
and by the grace of the Lord Jesus Christ.

Out of discord, bring harmony.
Out of chaos, bring order.
Out of tension, bring peace.
Out of anger, bring love.

CALLS TO WORSHIP

Leader:	We will honor the Lord at all times; God's praise shall always be on our lips.
People:	OUR SOULS WILL BOAST IN THE LORD; LET THE AFFLICTED HEAR AND REJOICE.
Leader:	Come, glorify the Lord with me.
People:	WE WILL EXALT GOD'S NAME TOGETHER!

— Adapted from Psalm 34:1-3

Leader:	May all people praise you, O God;
People:	MAY ALL THE PEOPLES PRAISE YOU.
Leader:	May the nations be glad and sing for joy,
People:	FOR YOU RULE THE PEOPLES JUSTLY AND GUIDE THE NATIONS OF THE EARTH.
Leader:	May the peoples praise you, O God,
People:	MAY ALL THE PEOPLES PRAISE YOU.

— Psalm 67:3-5, NIV

Let all the peoples praise the Lord,
let the nations be glad and sing for joy,
for God judges the peoples with equity,
and guides the nations upon earth.

— Adapted from Psalm 67:3-5

Leader:	Sing to the Lord a new song, for he has done marvelous things.
People:	PRAISE THE LORD, ALL PEOPLES ON EARTH, AND BREAK INTO SONGS OF JOY.
Leader:	With stringed instruments and with horns make a joyful noise before the King.
People:	PRAISE THE LORD, ALL PEOPLES ON EARTH, AND BREAK INTO SONGS OF JOY.
Leader:	Let the rivers clap their hands, let the hills sing together.
People:	PRAISE THE LORD, ALL PEOPLES ON EARTH, AND BREAK INTO SONGS OF JOY.
Leader:	For the Lord will judge the earth with righteousness and the peoples with justice.
People:	PRAISE THE LORD, ALL PEOPLES ON EARTH, AND BREAK INTO SONGS OF JOY.

— Adapted from Psalm 98

Come, bless the Lord,
all you servants of the Lord,
who stand by night in the house of the Lord.
Lift up your hands to the holy place,
and bless the Lord!

— Psalm 134:1-2

Blessed is the nation whose God is the Lord,
in whose homes there is love,
in whose courts there is justice,
in whose marketplace there is honesty,
in whose policies there is peace.

Leader: "Where two or three are gathered in my name," said Jesus, "I will be there to bless them."
People: WE ARE MORE THAN TWO OR THREE, AND WE ARE GATHERED IN JESUS' NAME.
Leader: Therefore we claim for ourselves the promise of his presence.
People: AND WE GATHER TO WORSHIP IN THE CONFIDENCE THAT HE STANDS AMONG US.

Proclaim liberty from the mountaintop,
announce freedom throughout the land,
guarantee justice for all the people
and deliverance for the oppressed,
for this is the will of the Lord.

INVOCATIONS

Leader: To you, O Lord, do we lift up our souls.
People: IN YOU, O GOD, DO WE TRUST.
Leader: Do not let us be put to shame,
People: NOR LET OUR ENEMIES TRIUMPH OVER US.
Leader: No one who hopes in you will ever be put to shame,
People: BUT THEY WILL BE PUT TO SHAME WHO ARE
WANTONLY TREACHEROUS.
Leader: Show us your ways, O Lord,
People: GUIDE US IN YOUR PATHS, AND TEACH US YOUR
TRUTH.

—Adapted from Psalm 25:1-5

On this Independence Day weekend it is right that we should gather in this house of worship, to make use of the freedom of worship which we enjoy in this great land.

We know that many believers around the world do not have this privilege, and we pray that we may never take this freedom for granted. May we use it in a way which is acceptable in your sight.

We come today with many problems and many prayers.
Some of us are troubled;
some of us are not feeling well;
some of us are grieving;
some of us are struggling with decisions;
some of us are living with disabilities.
Meet our needs, Lord, and help us find solutions;
but even more than that, help us to praise you
and to know that your Spirit is at work in our lives.

We thank you, God, for the open doors of this church,
made possible by the freedoms of this land
and the sacrifices of your people.
We thank you also for the open door to the throne of heaven,
made possible by the sacrifice of Christ
and maintained by the power of the Holy Spirit.
Hear our songs of praise as we enter the doors —
the doors of this sanctuary and the door to your presence,
and bless us as we come to the holy place.

O Lord of grace and goodness,
may what we *do here* fulfill your will;
may what we *say here* proclaim your glory;
and may what we *are here* be expressive of your Spirit's working.

We give thanks, Lord, for the privilege of worshipping in this house
of praise without harassment,
for the freedom to proclaim the truth without censorship,
and for the liberty to go out and witness publicly to our faith.
Enable us to use these freedoms responsibly and thankfully this
day.

We know, Lord, that we cannot learn from you unless we welcome
both your Word and Spirit. Grant us new insights as we open the
ancient documents, and help us to see their meaning for the
present. Prod us to action as we take our role of discipleship
seriously. May our minds catch a new vision as we are flooded with
your divine light.

We are thankful, Father, for the freedom we have to worship
according to the convictions of conscience, without fear of arrest
and without danger of recrimination in the business place or
school. As we worship today, may we become more worthy of the
privileges we enjoy.

PRAYERS OF CONFESSION

PRAYER OF CONFESSION

Leader: For the times we paid our duty to our country, but neglected our duty to you,

People: LORD, HAVE MERCY.

Leader: For the times we were conscientious about our duty to you, but neglected our obligations to country,

People: LORD, HAVE MERCY.

Leader: For the times we thought only of ourselves, neglecting both you and our fellow citizens,

People: LORD, HAVE MERCY.

WORDS OF ASSURANCE

The Word of the Lord to ancient Israel can be applied to our own country as well:
O nation, hope in the Lord!
For with the Lord there is steadfast love,
and with him is plenteous redemption.
For God will redeem our nation
from all its iniquities.

— Adapted from Psalm 130:7-8

PRAYER OF CONFESSION

Is it possible, Lord, that we get along so well because we never really take a stand? Could it be that people never raise their eyebrows at us simply because we try so hard to conform? Is it conceivable that others never ask about the hope that is in us because the evidence of that hope is not obvious? Could it be that people don't challenge our faith because they are not aware of that faith?

If these things are true, Lord, we stand humbled before you, begging that you will forgive our timidity and beseeching you to help strengthen the courage of our convictions.

WORDS OF ASSURANCE

May you be strengthened with all power,
according to his glorious might,
for all endurance and patience with joy.

— Colossians 1:11

PRAYER OF CONFESSION

(Suggestion: From a current newspaper or news magazine take headlines as topics of confession. For example:)
Leader: "Defense Contractor Indicted for Fraud."
People: FATHER, FORGIVE, AND HEAL OUR LAND.
Leader: "Racism Still Flourishing, Says Sociologist."
People: FATHER, FORGIVE, AND HEAL OUR LAND.
Leader: "Business Foreclosures Increase by 17%."
People: FATHER, FORGIVE, AND HEAL OUR LAND.
Leader: "Peace Talks Break Down Again."
People: FATHER, FORGIVE, AND HEAL OUR LAND. (etc.)

WORDS OF ASSURANCE

The word of the Lord which came to Solomon comes also to us: "If my people who are called by my name humble themselves, and pray and seek my face, and turn from their wicked ways, then I will hear from heaven, and will forgive their sin and heal their land."

— 2 Chronicles 7:14

PRAYER OF CONFESSION

We confess that as a nation you have sent us prophets, and we have often turned a deaf ear.

We have labeled them as fanatics, as troublemakers, and as extremists.

We have preferred to listen to those who proclaimed peace when there was no peace.

We have, by finding minor flaws, discounted their disturbing message.

We have ignored the prophetic pleas for justice, equality, and righteousness.

We have preferred our habits and our traditions to the way of the Lord.

Forgive us, O Lord, for closing our ears to your prophets, who to this day have little honor in their own country.

WORDS OF ASSURANCE

If we humble ourselves, and return to the Lord, the God of the nations will forgive us and restore us.

PRAYER OF CONFESSION

Leader: Holy God, before whom all the nations of the world will be judged — and are being judged,

People: HEAR OUR PRAYER OF CONFESSION.

Leader: For our nation's misuse and waste of natural resources; for the pollution of the good earth, the waters, and the sky,

People: HEAR OUR PRAYER FOR PARDON.

Leader: For our abuse of power, for our arrogance among the nations of the world, for our vast expenditures for weapons of destruction,

People: HEAR OUR PLEA FOR FORGIVENESS.

Leader: For our sins against humanity: for broken treaties with Native Americans, for the enslavement of Africans, for the imprisonment of Japanese Americans, for our neglect of the poor, for our destruction of the unborn,

People: HEAR OUR PRAYER OF CONFESSION FOR CORPORATE SIN.

Leader: For our trust in the gross national product, for our unbiblical pursuit of luxury, for our infatuation with things material,

People: HEAR OUR PRAYER FOR FORGIVENESS.

Leader: For the deterioration of our national moral tone, for the pollution of our airwaves, for the disintegration of our family structure, for our fascination with chemicals that alter the mind.

People: HEAR OUR PLEA FOR MERCY.

WORDS OF ASSURANCE

The Apostle Peter assures us that if we repent, if we turn, our sins will be blotted out, and times of refreshing will come from the presence of the Lord.

— Adapted from Acts 3:19

PRAYER OF CONFESSION

Forgive, O God of justice, the sins of our common life.
The cry of the needy falls upon ears that are closed.
The rich evade taxes which could help the destitute.
We trust in armaments and the threat of annihilation.
The great and the greedy devour the property of the poor.
Justice is tilted toward those who can buy it.
Remind us again, O God of the nations,
that righteousness exalts a nation,
but sin is a blight upon any people.

WORDS OF ASSURANCE

I will put my law within them, and I will write it on their hearts; and I
will be their God, and they shall be my people ... for I will forgive
their iniquity, and remember their sin no more.

— Jeremiah 31:33-34

LITANY OF CONFESSION AND INTERCESSION

Pastor: If we have ignored the prophets who have called for justice,

People: FORGIVE US AND HEAL OUR LAND.

Pastor: If we have made heroes of those who win by violence,

People: FORGIVE US AND HEAL OUR LAND.

Pastor: If we have allowed wealth to be the criterion of favor,

People: FORGIVE US AND HEAL OUR LAND.

Pastor: If we have closed our ears to the cries of the poor,

People: FORGIVE US AND HEAL OUR LAND.

Pastor: If we have allowed greed to devastate the beauty of our land,

People: FORGIVE US AND HEAL OUR LAND.

Pastor: If we have shrugged about corruption in high places,

People: FORGIVE US AND HEAL OUR LAND.

Pastor: If we have failed to use the privilege of the ballot,

People: FORGIVE US AND HEAL OUR LAND.

Pastor: If we have sat mute before the degenerating morality of our media,

People: FORGIVE US AND HEAL OUR LAND.

Pastor: If we have perpetuated historical patterns of discrimination,

People: FORGIVE US AND HEAL OUR LAND.

Pastor: If we have ridiculed the truly prophetic voices of our nation,

People: FORGIVE US AND HEAL OUR LAND.

WORDS OF ASSURANCE

As the Lord spoke to Solomon, so also he speaks to us: "If my people who are called by my name humble themselves, and pray and seek my face, and turn from their wicked ways, then I will hear from heaven, and will forgive their sin and heal their land."

— 2 Chronicles 7:14

PRAYER OF CONFESSION

When it comes to dealing with those who are limited, handicapped, and have special needs, we confess that we sometimes are uncomfortable and even neglectful. We have not shoved them down, but neither have we lifted them up. We have not taunted, but neither have we encouraged. We have not discriminated against, but neither have we advocated for. We have not made insensitive comments, but neither have we discouraged others from doing so. We have not told the disabled that they can't enter our church, our club, or our place of business; but neither have we made an extra effort to make it easy. Forgive, Lord, not only our sins of intention, but also our sins of neglect.

WORDS OF ASSURANCE

As Jesus said to the paralytic at Nazareth, he says to us today, "Take heart ... your sins are forgiven."

— Matthew 9:2

PRAYER OF CONFESSION

Forgive us, O Lord, if we have been unconcerned about the
spiritual and moral health of our great land:
if our pens have been unmoved;
if our votes have not been cast;
if our voices have been silent;
if our prayers have been selfish;
if our encouragement has not been expressed;
if our convictions have not been made known;
if our private commitment has never made the transition to public
    opinion.
Forgive our sins of silence, O Lord, and weave our faith into the
tapestry of our nation.

WORDS OF ASSURANCE

The sacrifice acceptable to God is a broken spirit; a broken and
contrite heart God will not despise.

— Adapted from Psalm 51:17

69

GENERAL PRAYERS

PRAYER OF THANKSGIVING
(For our land)

On this weekend in which we celebrate the anniversary of our country, we pause to give thanks for the many luxuries we enjoy in this land: for food in abundance; for comfortable homes; for the opportunity of receiving fair wages for our labor; for the luxury of vacation times; for clothing available in great variety; for automobiles and boats; for arts and entertainment; and for educational opportunities.

We are also grateful for the intangibles: for the freedom to worship according to our own conscience; for the freedom to read books of our own choosing; for the freedom to watch movies and plays of our own taste; and for the freedom from the constant barrage of government propaganda.

We are thankful for the right to inquire after the truth, no matter where the inquiry leads; for the freedom to write letters critical of the government; for the freedom to question the integrity of our leaders; for the right to do historical research; for the right to bring about change and reform and for the rights of a secret ballot.

PRAYER OF INTERCESSION
(For good influence in our land)

For all the influences for good in our land, we give you thanks:
— For townspeople who are willing to serve on the commissions and boards of local governments and schools, often with little pay and much criticism.
— For political leaders who are public servants in the best sense of the term, putting the good of the people before personal gain.
— For those who are the watchdogs of our democracy, insisting that our nation adhere to the principles of freedom guaranteed by the Constitution.
— For Christian believers in places of influence who bring their convictions to bear upon public policy.
— For the reformers of our republic who will not be content until our nation fully practices justice and promotes peace.
— For citizens who learn as much as they can about the issues of the day and who take the time to cast their ballots at public elections.

PRAYER OF THANKS
(For our freedoms)

God of both justice and mercy, we are grateful for the freedoms we enjoy in our country, and we pray that we may always use them in a positive and constructive manner.

For the freedom of the press we are grateful; and we commit ourselves to seeking truth and promoting decency in the printed word.

For the freedom of religion we are grateful; and we commit ourselves to living our faith in a manner both exemplary and forthright.

For the freedom of speech we are grateful; and we commit ourselves to speaking out for that which is right and good.

For the freedom to assemble we are grateful; and we commit ourselves to peace, harmony, and responsible living.

For the freedom of want we are grateful; and we commit ourselves to overcoming greed and sharing our surplus.

PRAYER OF INTERCESSION
(For those who are suffering for their faith)

Our thoughts and our prayers go out for those who are suffering for their faith. We think of villagers who have been attacked by angry people who were once their friends; of Christians who now have lost the only home they knew because they dared to forsake the traditional rituals.

We think of people whose faith has compelled them to speak out for justice and equality, thus putting them on a collision course with their government.

We think of children and young people in schools and colleges, young believers who have had to endure scorn because they had the courage to say No.

We think of adults who have lost jobs because they refused to carry out unethical policies, who have been ostracized from social groups because of their moral standards, who have been fired because they dared blow the whistle on their employers.

The Nation

OFFERTORY SENTENCES

When you have eaten your fill and have built fine houses and live in them, and when your herds and flocks have multiplied, and your silver and gold is multiplied, and all that you have is multiplied, then do not exalt yourself, forgetting the Lord your God.
— Deuteronomy 8:12-14

He who closes his ear to the cry of the poor will himself cry out and not be heard.
— Proverbs 21:13

On this Sunday in which we anticipate the celebration of our nation's independence, it is fitting that we acknowledge our obligation to both God and country. "Give to Caesar what is Caesar's," said Jesus, " and to God what is God's."
— Matthew 22:21, NIV

As we present these gifts, we are conscious of the dual authorities of our lives; how we owe allegiance both to our country and to the kingdom of God. May we be faithful in our obligations: honest in paying taxes and generous in sharing our tithes.

In the course of our lives we have many obligations: to pay our taxes; to pay for our food, shelter, and clothing; and to retire the other debts which we owe. Now, as we present these gifts, we acknowledge a further obligation — a commitment to the God who has created, redeemed, and sustained us.

As we are loyal to our government on earth by paying taxes and personally supporting and encouraging elected officials, so let us be loyal to the earthly rule of Jesus Christ by sharing our free-will offerings and by our personal and prayer support of those who represent us around the world.

OFFERTORY PRAYERS

To you, O Lord, do we raise our thanks for the wealth of this great land — for the produce of farm and market, for the products of business and industry, for the investments of trade and commerce. Help us, individually and corporately, to be honest, just, and responsible caretakers of all we have received.

Enable us to see that the blessings we enjoy as citizens of this great land are meant to be shared for the good of all mankind and for the glory of your name.

As citizens of this country we pay taxes as our fair share of the services we enjoy and the obligations we have to others. As citizens of your heavenly rule we also recognize the benefits we enjoy and wish to share them with others. Receive these gifts as we give them freely and gladly.

Out of our abundance — both material and spiritual — we now share with a needy world. As we have generously received, so we generously give.

We are humbled by the thought that our offerings represent very little sacrifice when compared to those given by many of our brothers and sisters from other parts of the world. So we give in humility, acknowledging the commitment of others.

As we give, we recognize that we have obligations both to the kingdom of God and to the structures of authority here on earth. Help us to be good citizens of both — in our obedience, in our support, and in our efforts for justice and freedom.

BENEDICTIONS

Do justice,
love kindness,
and walk humbly with your God.

— Adapted from Micah 6:8

May the Lord bless you and your children after you,
granting prosperity and freedom,
and peace in our time.

As you go, during this coming week,
to your homes, your schools, your places of work and business,
do so with a new outlook,
a new vibrancy,
and a new sense of direction,
for God has cleared your vision and strengthened your heart.

May the word of the Lord prevail in our land and may the Lord heal
our troubled world, as we look to the time when the kingdoms of
this world will become the kingdom of our God.

May the love of the Father, who watches over you,
may the grace of the Son, who walks beside you,
may the presence of the Holy Spirit, who lives within you,
be yours, now and forever more.

Leader: Having heard the good news,
People: WE WILL SHARE IT WITH OUR FRIENDS.
Leader: Having experienced God's love,
People: WE WILL EXPRESS IT IN OUR DAILY CONTACTS.
Leader: Having worshiped the Lord here,
People: WE WILL PRAISE HIM IN THE STREETS OF OUR
LIVES.

74

CALLS TO WORSHIP

Current Thanksgiving Proclamation
and/or

Leader: We will bless the Lord at all times;
People: HIS PRAISE SHALL CONTINUALLY BE IN MY MOUTH.
Leader: Our souls make their boast in the Lord,
People: LET THE HUMBLE HEAR AND REJOICE.
Leader: Proclaim with us the greatness of God,
People: AND LET US EXALT HIS NAME TOGETHER!

— Adapted from Psalm 34:1-3

God cares for the land and waters it,
he enriches it abundantly.
The streams of God are filled with water
to provide the people with grain.
God has crowned the year with bounty,
and our wagons overflow with abundance.
The grasslands of the desert overflow,
the hills are clothed with gladness.
The meadows are covered with flocks
and the valleys are mantled with grain;
they shout for joy and sing.
Come, let us give thanks unto God.

— Adapted from Psalm 65:9-13

The pastures of the wilderness overflow,
the hills gird themselves with joy,
the meadows clothe themselves with flocks,
the valleys deck themselves with grain,
they shout and sing together for joy.

— Psalm 65:12-13

Leader: The earth has yielded its increase;
People: GOD, OUR GOD, HAS BLESSED US.
Leader: May God continue to bless us;
People: LET ALL THE ENDS OF THE EARTH REVERE HIM.

— Psalm 67:6-7

75

Leader: It is good to give thanks to the Lord,
People: TO SING PRAISES TO THE NAME OF THE MOST
          HIGH,
Leader: To declare his steadfast love in the morning,
People: AND HIS FAITHFULNESS BY NIGHT.
                              — Adapted from Psalm 92:1-2

Leader: Come, let us sing for joy to the Lord;
          let us shout aloud to the Rock of our salvation.
People: LET US COME BEFORE HIM WITH THANKSGIVING
          AND EXTOL HIM WITH MUSIC AND SONG.
Leader: For the Lord is the great God,
          the great King above all gods.
People: IN HIS HAND ARE THE DEPTHS OF THE EARTH,
          AND THE MOUNTAIN PEAKS BELONG TO HIM.
Leader: The sea is his, for he made it,
          and his hands formed the dry land.
People: COME, LET US BOW DOWN IN WORSHIP, LET US
          KNEEL BEFORE THE LORD OUR MAKER;
Leader: For he is our God
Unison: AND WE ARE THE PEOPLE OF HIS PASTURE, THE
          FLOCK UNDER HIS CARE.
                              — Psalm 95:1-7, NIV

Pastor: Enter his gates with thanksgiving, and his courts with
          praise!
People: GIVE THANKS TO HIM, BLESS HIS NAME!
Pastor: For the Lord is good;
People: HIS STEADFAST LOVE ENDURES FOR EVER, AND
          HIS FAITHFULNESS TO ALL GENERATIONS.
                              — Psalm 100:4, 5

Leader: O give thanks to the Lord, for he is good;
People: FOR HIS STEADFAST LOVE ENDURES FOR EVER!
Leader: Let them thank the Lord for his steadfast love,
People: FOR HIS WONDERFUL WORKS TO HUMANKIND!
Leader: For he satisfies the thirsty,
People: AND THE HUNGRY HE FILLS WITH GOOD THINGS.
                                                — Psalm 107:1, 8-9

Pastor: Let us thank the Lord for his steadfast love,
People: FOR HIS WONDERFUL WORKS TO HUMANKIND.
Pastor: Let us offer thanksgiving sacrifices,
People: AND TELL OF GOD'S DEEDS WITH SONGS OF JOY.
                                          — Adapted from Psalm 107:21-22

Leader: O give thanks to the Lord, for he is good,
People: FOR HIS STEADFAST LOVE ENDURES FOR EVER.
Leader: O give thanks to the God of gods,
People: FOR HIS STEADFAST LOVE ENDURES FOR EVER.
Leader: O give thanks to the Lord of lords,
People: FOR HIS STEADFAST LOVE ENDURES FOR EVER.
Leader: O give thanks to the God of heaven,
People: FOR HIS STEADFAST LOVE ENDURES FOR EVER.
                                                — Psalm 136:1-3, 26

It is a good thing to acknowledge the Lord,
and to give thanks to our redeemer;
to come before his throne with singing,
and to join his people in praise.

Thanksgiving

INVOCATIONS

Leader: We will praise you, O Lord, with all the heart,
before the gods we will sing your praise.
People: WE WILL BOW DOWN TOWARD YOUR HOLY
TEMPLE AND WILL PRAISE YOUR NAME
FOR YOUR LOVE AND YOUR FAITHFULNESS,
Leader: For you have exalted above all things
your name and your word.
People: WHEN WE CALLED, YOU ANSWERED US,
YOU MADE US BOLD AND STOUTHEARTED.
— Adapted from Psalm 138:1-3

Leader: God of night and day, summer and winter, seedtime
and harvest,
People: HEAR OUR PRAYERS AND ACCEPT OUR PRAISE.
Leader: God of music and moaning, dancing and weeping,
People: RECEIVE OUR THANKSGIVING AND REMEMBER
OUR NEEDS.
Leader: God of crashing seas and silent shadows,
People: HONOR OUR WORSHIP AND LIFT UP OUR SOULS.

We are grateful, Lord God, for the love and laughter we experience
as families as we gather around tables overflowing with food. We
are grateful also for the love and laughter we experience as the
family of God, as we gather around this table of your presence and
celebrate the goodness of your grace.

We have gathered once again, as our custom is,
to raise our prayers and songs of thanks
on this day of national thanksgiving.
May this day be the expression of conviction,
and not merely the observance of a custom.
May our words represent the gratitude of an overflowing heart
and may we direct our attention to you, the Giver,
instead of merely indulging ourselves, the receivers.

78

We approach you, heavenly Father,
as the source of all life,
as the origin of all things bright and beautiful,
as the creator of all light and love,
and as the father of our Lord Jesus Christ.
Receive our honor and praise,
and share anew with us the joy of your presence.

Leader: Jesus Christ, whose teachings astonished the crowds
          on the hillside,
People: TEACH US THE WORDS OF ETERNAL LIFE.
Leader: Jesus Christ, who promised new birth to Nicodemus,
People: CREATE A MIRACLE OF NEW STIRRINGS WITHIN
          US.
Leader: Jesus Christ, who healed ten men of leprosy,
People: HEAL US IN BODY AND SOUL.
Leader: Jesus Christ, who asked, "Where are the nine?"
People: ACCEPT OUR FERVENT THANKSGIVING AND OUR
          PRAISE.

O Lord God,
creator of mind,
author of truth,
giver of life,
designer of love,
accept now our humble worship and grateful prayers
as we gather on this special day
of thanksgiving and praise.

God of seedtime and harvest,
summer and winter,
light and darkness,
we are grateful that in the cycles of your mercy
you have again brought us to this day of thanksgiving.
Accept now our praise for the continuing evidence of your power
and love.

You have created us in your image.
You have cleansed us from our guilt.
You have granted us the miracle of rebirth.
You have provided us with guidance for daily living.
Therefore it is with thanksgiving that we gather here,
and with anticipation that we approach your throne.

It is right, Father, that we should celebrate Thanksgiving in your house as well as around our own tables. Accept our thanks as we celebrate here the world you have created, the provisions you share with us daily, and the life you have given us through Jesus Christ.

PRAYERS OF CONFESSION

PRAYER OF CONFESSION

All: FOR THE SIN OF THANKLESSNESS, WE ASK YOUR PARDON.

Leader: We have received our gifts with joy,

People: BUT WE HAVE FORGOTTEN THE GIVER.

Leader: We have taken credit for our successes,

People: BUT HAVE FAILED TO ACKNOWLEDGE THE ROLE OF OTHERS.

Leader: We have cried to you in time of need.

People: BUT HAVE NEGLECTED YOU IN TIMES OF PROSPERITY.

Leader: We have courted the favor of others,

People: THEN, HAVING RECEIVED, WE HAVE TURNED AWAY.

All: FOR THE SIN OF THANKLESSNESS, WE ASK YOUR PARDON.

WORDS OF ASSURANCE

Leader: We believe that God is love,

People: AND THAT IF WE CONFESS OUR SINS, HE IS FAITHFUL AND JUST, AND WILL FORGIVE US OUR SINS AND CLEANSE US FROM ALL UNRIGHTEOUSNESS.

— Adapted from 1 John 1:9

PRAYER OF CONFESSION

Our heavenly Father, we confess that we have not been as grateful as the cleansed leper who returned to give thanks.

Sometimes we forget about you, once the crisis is past. Often we just think we are too busy. At other times we simply fail to see your hand in our healing. And sometimes we have continued to be preoccupied with the problems that remain instead of being grateful for those which have been solved.

Most seriously, we have often taken our health and our well-ordered lives for granted, failing to thank you for the rhythmic beating of our hearts, and for the food on our tables, and for the comforts we enjoy.

Grant us, we pray, not only the benefit of your generosity and your healing, but also the inner miracle of the soul which seeks to express its heartfelt thanks.

WORDS OF ASSURANCE

Even as we confess our thanklessness,
we express our gratitude,
for God is a gracious God
who looks with compassion upon our struggles
and forgives us when we miss the mark.

PRAYER OF CONFESSION

Leader: If our prayers of petition have been more frequent and fervent than our prayers of thanksgiving,

People: FORGIVE OUR THOUGHTLESSNESS AND HEAR OUR WORDS OF THANKS.

Leader: If after feverish petition we received what we asked, then turned away to other matters without so much as a nod of thanks,

People: FORGIVE OUR THANKLESSNESS AND ACCEPT OUR BELATED PRAYER OF GRATITUDE.

Leader: If we have credited ourselves for our successes while blaming others for our setbacks,

People: FORGIVE OUR SINS AND HEAL US OF OUR ARRO-GANCE.

Leader: If during the course of the day we do a lot more complaining than we do appreciating,

People: FORGIVE OUR INGRATITUDE AND OPEN OUR EYES TO THE GOOD THAT SURROUNDS US.

WORDS OF ASSURANCE

Likewise the Spirit helps us in our weakness; for we do not know how to pray as we ought, but that very Spirit intercedes with sighs too deep for words.

— Romans 8:26

PRAYER OF CONFESSION

God of generosity, in whom we live and move and have our being, we confess that we have sometimes accepted your gifts without so much as a nod in your direction. We have often complained more than we have complimented; we have been more ready to deprecate than we have been to appreciate. We have considered the cup to be half empty rather than half full. We have taken credit for the good while passing on the blame for the bad. Forgive our sins of forgetfulness, thoughtlessness, and thanklessness; and help us to live with prayers of thanksgiving on our lips.

WORDS OF ASSURANCE

God, who is rich in mercy, out of the great love with which he loved us ... made us alive together with Christ.
— Ephesians 2:4, 5

PRAYER OF CONFESSION

Leader: If, after we have received, we have neglected to show our gratitude,
People: FORGIVE US AND HELP US TO BE TRULY GRATEFUL.
Leader: If, after having received, we have demanded even more,
People: FORGIVE US AND HELP US TO BE TRULY THANKFUL.
Leader: If, after having received, we have been hesitant to share,
People: FORGIVE US AND HELP US TO BE TRULY THANKFUL.
Leader: If, after having received, we have defaced and destroyed,
People: FORGIVE US AND HELP US TO BE TRULY THANKFUL.
Leader: If, after having received, we have given all the credit to ourselves,
People: FORGIVE US AND HELP US TO BE TRULY THANKFUL.

WORDS OF ASSURANCE

A new heart I will give you, and a new spirit I will put within you.
— Ezekiel 36:26

LITANIES OF THANKSGIVING

Leader: For all the gifts you have given us,
for the life you have shared with us,
for the world in which we live,
People: WE PRAISE YOU, O GOD.
Leader: For the work we are enabled to do,
for the knowledge we are privileged to learn,
for the pleasure we are permitted to experience,
People: WE THANK YOU, O GOD.
Leader: For the order and constancy of nature,
for the beauty and bounty of the earth,
for day and night, summer and winter,
seedtime and harvest,
People: WE BLESS YOU, O GOD.
Leader: For the autumn and all its color,
for the fertility of the earth, the coolness of the rain,
and the warmth of the sunshine,
for the harvest and its abundance provisions,
People: WE HONOR YOU, O GOD.
Leader: For the comforts and gladness of life,
for families and friends,
for the warmth of love,
People: WE PRAISE YOU, O GOD.
Leader: For the blessings of civilization,
for the orderliness of government,
for the arts and the sciences,
People: WE BLESS YOU, O GOD.
Leader: And most of all,
for the gift of your Son, Jesus Christ,
for his life, death, resurrection, and coming again,
for the presence of the Holy Spirit,
People: WE THANK YOU, O GOD.
Leader: For the open lines of prayer,
for peace of heart and inspiration of mind,
for the honor of sharing your grace with others,
People: WE PRAISE YOU, O GOD.

Leader: For the season of planting and the season of harvesting,
People: WE THANK YOU , O LORD.
Leader: For seasons of laughter and seasons of tears,
People: WE THANK YOU, O LORD.
Leader: For the companionship of friends and the challenge of adversaries,
People: WE THANK YOU , O LORD.
Leader: For times of sociability and times of solitude,
People: WE THANK YOU , O LORD.
Leader: For the blessings of receiving and the fulfillment of giving,
People: WE THANK YOU , O LORD.
Leader: For the excitement of new discoveries and the security of old haunts,
People: WE THANK YOU , O LORD.
Leader: For the gift of pleasure and the warning of pain,
People: WE THANK YOU , O LORD.
Leader: For the exhilaration of freedom and the discipline of law,
People: WE THANK YOU , O LORD.
Leader: For the exuberance of youth and the wisdom of maturity,
People: WE THANK YOU , O LORD.
Leader: For the warmth of intimacy and the freedom of self-realization,
People: WE THANK YOU , O LORD.
Leader: For the joys of victory and the lessons of defeat,
People: WE THANK YOU , O LORD.
Leader: For the satisfaction of work completed and the challenge of tasks yet undone,
People: WE THANK YOU , O LORD.
Leader: For the peace of forgiveness and the restlessness of imperfection,
People: WE THANK YOU , O LORD.
Leader: For a time to anticipate and a time to appreciate,
People: WE THANK YOU , O LORD.

Leader: Enter into his gates with thanksgiving,
and into his courts with praise.
Be thankful to him, and bless his name.

People: FOR SEEDTIME AND HARVEST,
FOR SPRING RAINS AND SUMMER HEAT,
FOR FRESH FRUIT AND RIPENING GRAIN,

Leader: O Lord, we thank you.

People: FOR ROSE-RED SUNSETS AND STARLIT NIGHTS,
FOR HILLS CLOTHED IN TREES AND FOR PLAINS
WHICH STRETCH TO THE HORIZON,
FOR BUTTERFLIES AND ZEBRAS,

Leader: O Father, we praise you.

People: FOR THE TIMES WE LAUGHED UNTIL OUR SIDES
ACHED,
FOR THE FRIENDS WHO SAT WITH US LATE INTO
THE NIGHT,
FOR FAMILY MEMBERS WHO SURROUND US WITH
LOVE,

Leader: O God, we thank you.

People: FOR EACH DAY'S WORK AND EACH NIGHT'S REST,
FOR THE EXHILARATION OF MIND AND BODY,
FOR THE RAINBOW AFTER THE STORM,

Leader: O Lord, we thank you.

People: FOR THE MIRACLE OF SALVATION AND THE
PRIVILEGE OF PRAYER,
FOR THE GIFTS OF THE SPIRIT AND THE EVER-
LASTING ARMS,
FOR THE PROMISE OF AN ETERNAL TOMORROW,

Leader: O Lord, we praise you.

People: FOR THE NATION WHICH HAS NURTURED US,
FOR THE RIGHTS OF THE BALLOT BOX AND THE
PUBLIC MEETING,
FOR THE FREEDOMS OF WORSHIP AND DISSENT,

Leader: O Father, we thank you.

People: FOR THE TIMES WE NARROWLY ESCAPED
DANGER,
FOR THE TIMES WE COULD HAVE CHOSEN EVIL,
BUT DIDN'T,
FOR THE GIFT OF FAITH WHICH HAS ENABLED US
TO SURVIVE EACH CRISIS,

Leader: O God, we thank you.

87

Leader: For the satisfaction of labor and the refreshment of leisure,
People: WE THANK YOU, O LORD.
Leader: For the heat of midday and the coolness of the evening,
People: WE THANK YOU, O LORD.
Leader: For the briskness of winter and the brightness of summer,
People: WE THANK YOU, O LORD.
Leader: For the anticipation of seedtime and the completion of harvest,
People: WE THANK YOU, O LORD.
Leader: For the challenge of new tasks and the familiarity of old ones,
People: WE THANK YOU, O LORD.
Leader: For the affirmation of strengths and the correction of faults,
People: WE THANK YOU, O LORD.
Leader: For the closeness of companionship and the peace of solitude,
People: WE THANK YOU, O LORD.
Leader: For the celebration of triumphs and the lessons of setbacks,
People: WE THANK YOU, O LORD.
Leader: For the blessings of plenty and the testings of poverty,
People: WE THANK YOU, O LORD.
Leader: For the companionship of your Spirit and the wisdom of your Word,
People: WE THANK YOU, O LORD.
Leader: For the comfort of your promises and the challenge of your commandments,
People: WE THANK YOU, O LORD.
Leader: For the privilege of receiving and the fulfillment of giving,
People: WE THANK YOU, O LORD.
Leader: For the celebration of life and the promises beyond death,
People: WE THANK YOU, O LORD.

Leader: For the world you have given us,
             for mountains and seas,
             for butterflies and elephants,
             for sunny days and moonlit nights,
People: WE THANK YOU, O LORD.
Leader: For the nation in which we are privileged to live,
             for its peace and prosperity,
             for its guarantee of human rights,
             for its opportunities and freedoms,
People: WE THANK YOU, O LORD.
Leader: For the families we enjoy,
             for the vibrancy of young life,
             for the security of belonging,
             for the pleasures of love,
People: WE THANK YOU, O LORD.
Leader: For the work you have given us to do,
             for keenness of mind and strength of arm,
             for new challenges and possibilities,
             for financial and personal rewards,
People: WE THANK YOU, O LORD.
Leader: For the benefits we enjoy as Christian believers,
             for the cleansing of forgiveness,
             for the fellowship of the church,
             for the presence and power of the Spirit,
             for the hope of life eternal,
People: WE THANK YOU, O LORD.

Leader: For the rhythms of day and night,
            for summer and winter,
            for seedtime and harvest,
People: MAY GOD BE PRAISED.
Leader: For food which nourishes,
            for clothing which warms and enhances,
            and for homes which give us comfort,
People: MAY GOD BE PRAISED.
Leader: For the harmonies of music,
            for the colors of art,
            for the adventures of books,
People: MAY GOD BE PRAISED.
Leader: For the diversity of the human race,
            for the traditions of clan,
            for the richness of culture,
People: MAY GOD BE PRAISED.
Leader: For the wisdom of scholars,
            for the creativity of artists,
            for the boldness of leaders,
People: MAY GOD BE PRAISED.
Leader: For the beauty of love,
            for the chatter of children,
            for the bright promise of youth,
People: MAY GOD BE PRAISED.
Leader: For a nation which is free,
            for laws which are just,
            for peace in our time,
People: MAY GOD BE PRAISED.
Leader: For times of high challenge
            for times of structured sameness,
            for times of recreation and renewal,
People: MAY GOD BE PRAISED.
Leader: For disciplines which strengthen,
            for difficulties which challenge,
            for disappointments which humble,
People: MAY GOD BE PRAISED.
Leader: For the light that shines in darkness,
            for the joy that comes in the morning,
            for the rainbow after the storm,
People: MAY GOD BE PRAISED.
Leader: For the life and work of Jesus Christ,
            for the sacrifice of the cross,
            for the reality of the resurrection,
People: MAY GOD BE PRAISED.
Leader: For the truths that transform us,
            for the church which sustains us,
            for the providential care that surrounds us,
People: MAY GOD BE PRAISED.
Leader: For the cleansing of forgiveness,
            for the satisfaction of service,
            for the promise of life which never ends.
People: MAY GOD BE PRAISED.

90

Leader: For the world you have given us, we give you thanks:
People: FOR THE SEQUENCE OF SEASONS,
         THE GLORY OF MOUNTAINS,
         THE FERTILITY OF SOIL,
         SKIES THAT ARE BLUE AND CLOUDS THAT BRING
           RAIN,
         A WORLD ALIVE WITH THE SOUNDS OF LIFE.
Leader: For the joys of family, we praise you:
People: FOR THE SOUNDS OF LAUGHTER,
         THE SHARING OF NEWS,
         THE CONFIDENCE OF BELONGING,
         THE COMFORT OF MUTUAL SYMPATHY,
         THE PLEASURES OF AFFECTION.
Leader: For the challenges of our work, we give you thanks:
People: FOR TALENTS AND GIFTS INBORN,
         STRENGTHS OF BODY AND MIND,
         THE SATISFACTIONS OF ACCOMPLISHMENT.
Leader: For the privileges of freedom, we are thankful:
People: FOR THOSE IN OUR WORLD WHO DEFEND HUMAN
           RIGHTS,
         ONGOING STRUGGLES AGAINST TYRANNY,
         THE POWER OF THE BALLOT,
         WORSHIP WITHOUT RESTRAINT OR RECRIMI-
           NATION.
Leader: For the pleasures of mind and will, we praise you:
People: FOR THE EXCITEMENT OF DISCOVERY,
         THE HARMONIES OF MUSIC,
         THE MIRACLES OF MEMORY AND IMAGINATION,
         THE POSSIBILITIES AND DANGERS OF CHOICE.
Leader: For the comforts and challenges of faith, we give
           thanks:
People: FOR THE EXAMPLE AND ATONEMENT OF JESUS
           CHRIST,
         THE INWARD STRENGTHENING OF THE HOLY
           SPIRIT,
         THE SUPPORT AND LOVE OF FELLOW BELIEVERS,
         AND THE PROMISE OF LIFE ETERNAL.

91

GENERAL PRAYERS

PRAYER OF THANKS
(For the faithfulness of God)

We address you, Lord, as a faithful friend, as a compassionate helper, and as a constant companion. We are grateful for the hope you bring to our lives. Even when we have let you down, you did not give up on us. You have walked with us both in the sunshine and in the shadows.

You have blessed us with human companionship, and you have enriched our lives with laughter and beauty. When we were lonely, you sent someone to talk with us, and when we were sorrowful you sent someone to hear us. When we were happy you gave us someone to share our joy.

You have given us a land of great abundance, and few of us have ever gone to bed hungry. You have given us a land of unequaled freedom, and we express our opinions without fear of reprisal.

Above all, you have given us a reason for living and a reason for dying. You have saved us, body and soul, and have given us the assurance that you love us and have a plan for our lives.

PRAYER OF THANKS
(For the disciplines of life)

We know, Lord, that we sometimes squirm under the disciplines of life. We complain because of constraints placed upon us, and we rebel because we feel we are losing our freedom. Yet, when we try to see the whole picture, we realize that these disciplines can have a positive impact on our lives.

We are grateful for the discipline of work — for time clocks that motivate us to be prompt, for supervisors who draw from us our best, for demands which enhance our self-respect.

We are grateful for the disciplines of family — for those who expect much from us, for those who demand fidelity, for those who require obedience and respect.

We are grateful for the disciplines of learning — for the knowledge that comes only through diligence, for the insights which come only when ignorance is swept away.

We are grateful for the disciplines of faith — for the commandments of the law, for the high standards of the gospel, and for the example of Jesus Christ.

We are grateful even for the discipline of suffering, for through suffering we come to experience trust, and through trust we have learned how to hope.

PRAYER OF THANKS
(For the things we take for granted)

Hear our prayer, giver of all good and perfect things, for those aspects of your creation which we so often take for granted.

For the air we breathe, for the food we eat, for the water we drink.

For the ability to see, to hear, to feel, and to taste.

For the rhythms of day and night, summer and winter, sunshine and rain.

For the gift of life itself; for the mystery of consciousness, for the intricacies of the mind, and for the deep yearnings of the soul.

For all of these things, which are so basic to our existence, yet are so unconsciously accepted and experienced, we raise our prayer of thanks.

PRAYER OF THANKS
(For the functions of our bodies)

Hear our prayer of thanksgiving for bodies which are wonderfully and fearfully made, for the intricacy of your handiwork which we usually just take for granted.

We are grateful for a heart that keeps on beating without our direction; for eyes that focus and blink without our thought; for hands that reach out and grasp; for ears that hear the voices of love and the sounds of music; for the sense of touch that gives pleasure and warns of harm; for the complicated processes of digestion and assimilation which go on without our awareness; and for the wonders of a nervous system which keeps us in touch both with ourselves and with the outside world.

When some of these evidences of your handiwork do not work as well as we think they should, help us to realize our dependence on you and the transitory nature of our lives.

PRAYER OF THANKS
(For those who enrich our lives)

We thank you, O God, for the people who enrich our lives;
— for those who are always willing to be a sounding board;
— for friends who accept us for what we are;
— for competitors who bring out the best in us;
— for critics who, while irritating us, challenge us to prove them wrong;
— for counselors, teachers, and pastors who share good advice;
— for all those who love us and care for us;
— for those who set an example worthy to be followed;
— for those whose moral sensitivity pricks our conscience and challenges our self-indulgence.

PRAYER OF THANKS
(For work)

Receive our prayer of thanks for the strength of body, the acuteness of mind, and the stamina of will which enable us to earn a living.

Receive our prayer of thanks for the economic system of this country which gives us the opportunity to choose our vocation, to receive a free public education, and to move beyond our present situation in life. Where there are inequities, inspire us to help make them right.

Receive our prayer of thanks for those whose labors blend together with our own work to create a society which is mutually beneficial and supportive. Help us to realize that not one of us is independent; that every day we rely on each other to provide the essentials and the niceties of life.

OFFERTORY SENTENCES

The words of Moses to the people of Israel before they entered the promised land apply to us as well: "Take heed lest you forget the Lord your God, by not keeping his commandments and his ordinances and his statutes which I command you this day: lest, when you have eaten and are full, and have built goodly houses and live in them, and when your herds and flocks multiply, and your silver and gold is multiplied, and all that you have is multiplied, then your heart be lifted up, and you forget the Lord your God."

— Deuteronomy 8:11-14

Beware lest you say in your heart, "My power and the might of my hand have gotten me this wealth." You shall remember the Lord your God, for it is he who gives you power to get wealth.

— Deuteronomy 8:17-18

We remember the words of the Patriarch Joshua: "Choose this day whom you will serve ... but as for me and my house, we will serve the Lord" (Josh. 24:14-15). When we set a priority for ourselves, we are also setting an example for our families. With this in mind, let us present our offerings.

Offer to God a sacrifice of thanksgiving, and pay your vows to the Most High.

— Psalm 50:14

Make vows to the Lord your God, and perform them;
let all who are around him bring gifts
to the one who is awesome.

— Psalm 76:11

As we present these offerings of thanksgiving, let us ponder the question of Jesus: "Were not ten cleansed? Where are the nine?"

— Luke 17:17

"People must think of us as Christ's servants, stewards entrusted with the mysteries of God. What is expected of stewards is that each one should be found worthy of his trust."
— 1 Corinthians 4:1-2, Jerusalem Bible

You will be enriched in every way for your great generosity, which will produce thanksgiving to God through us; for the rendering of this ministry not only supplies the needs of the saints but also overflows with many thanksgivings to God.
— 2 Corinthians 9:11, 12

As our offering is received, let us use this opportunity to reinforce our words with our deeds; to say with our hands what we are saying with our mouths; to express outwardly what we are feeling inwardly.

As we give, let us praise God —
praise God for all we have received,
and praise God for all we are privileged to share.

OFFERTORY PRAYERS

Father, you have been most generous in your care for us. You have provided not only the necessities of life, but many of its luxuries as well. Moreover, you have satisfied the needs of our souls for this life and for the life to come. Receive these gifts as tangible expressions of our gratitude.

Help us, Lord, to express our thanksgiving through godliness and through contentment, always seeing who we are as being much more important than what we have.

So often do we ask for your blessings, and so seldom do we thank you for them. Receive our thanks as we express it both in word and in an act of sacrifice.

We have expressed our thanksgiving with the thoughts of our minds, the songs of our mouths, and the prayers of our lips. Now we express our thanksgiving with the gifts of our hands and the sacrifices of our lives. Receive them all, we pray, in the name of the Christ who has given us every reason to be thankful.

Leader: For the abundance we enjoy,
               and for the challenges we face,
People: WE GIVE THANKS, O LORD.
Leader: For the satisfaction of earning
               and the fulfillment of sharing,
People: WE GIVE THANKS, O LORD.
Leader: For the delight of self-indulgence
               and the challenge of self-denial,
People: WE GIVE THANKS, O LORD.

We have expressed out gratitude with our songs,
and we have thanked you in our prayers.
Receive now the gratitude of our gifts
and prepare us to thank you through service.

Accept these offerings as an expression of gratitude:
gratitude for the necessities and comforts we enjoy,
gratitude for life itself,
gratitude for the healing of our bodies,
and gratitude for the healing of our souls.

We can express our thanksgiving with our lips, but we can say
"thank you" even more convincingly with our hands. Receive these
gifts, we pray, as concrete evidence of our gratitude.

You have blessed us with good things,
    with food and clothing and shelter,
    and with much that adds to our pleasure and comfort.
Bless us, we pray, with only a few things more:
    with hearts that are grateful
    and with hands that are generous.

We are grateful, Father, for the health of body, the clarity of mind,
the resources of our land, and the opportunities of our society
which have made these gifts possible. Receive them, we pray, with
our thanks.

These gifts represent the toil of our hands, the sweat of our brows,
the ingenuity of our minds, and the use of our talents. Receive
them with our thanks; for our hands, our minds, and our talents
have first come from you.

BENEDICTIONS

"God will supply every need of yours according to his riches in glory in Christ Jesus. To our God and Father be glory for ever and ever."

— Philippians 4:19-20

Remember, there is great gain in godliness with contentment.
We brought nothing into the world,
and it is certain that we can carry nothing out.
But if we have food and clothing,
let us be content.

— Adapted from 1 Timothy 6:6-8

In your difficulties,
    practice perseverance.
In your sorrow,
    practice trust.
And in your success,
    practice thanksgiving.

May each of your days
be a thanksgiving day,
empty of complaints,
filled with gratitude,
punctuated by acts of sharing,
and brightened with a smile.

As you leave this sanctuary of worship,
may your life be a hymn of praise
and may your daily walk be a prayer of thanksgiving.

Go in peace, and put into practice your thanksgiving.
Support causes which are changing the world.
Use responsibly what God has given you.
Preserve the resources and beauty of God's world.
Have compassion on the poor, and walk in harmony with all.

As you leave this house of worship
may your life be a symphony of praise,
and may your words be a song of thanksgiving.

Remember that you are a people bought with a price,
consecrated, set apart,
bearing the name of Christ,
called out for both salvation and service.

CALLS TO WORSHIP

Praise the Lord!
Sing to the Lord a new song,
his praise in the assembly of the faithful!

— Psalm 149:1

Leader: The victory of the Lord is near.
People: PREPARE IN THE WILDERNESS A WAY FOR THE LORD.
Leader: His salvation is already upon us.
People: MAKE A HIGHWAY ACROSS THE DESERT FOR OUR GOD.
Leader: Our ruler will claim his rightful domain
People: THE GLORY OF THE LORD WILL BE REVEALED.
Leader: God will rule with justice and with love.
People: AND ALL THE PEOPLES OF THE EARTH WILL SEE IT.

— Adapted from Isaiah 40:3-5

Leader: With what shall we come before the Lord? Shall we come with sacrifices?
People: NO, HE HAS SHOWED US WHAT IS GOOD.
Leader: And what is good in God's eyes?
People: THAT WE DO JUSTICE,
AND LOVE KINDNESS,
AND WALK HUMBLY WITH OUR GOD.

— Adapted from Micah 6:6-8

With what shall I come before the Lord,
and bow myself before God on high?
He has told you, O mortal, what is good;
and what does the Lord require of you
but to do justice, and to love kindness,
and to walk humbly with your God?

— Micah 6:6, 8

103

Leader: God has shown us what is good.
         Do you know what he requires of us?
People: YES, WE MUST ACT JUSTLY, LOVE KINDNESS, AND
         WALK HUMBLY WITH OUR GOD.
Leader: God's desire is that justice may roll down like the
         waters,
People: AND RIGHTEOUSNESS LIKE AN OVERFLOWING
         STREAM.
                            — Adapted from Micah 6:8, Amos 5:24

God calls us to play an important role in the life of planet earth. Through Christ, he has called us to be lights in the present darkness and salt in the current state of decay. Let us, in this hour of worship, dedicate ourselves anew to our high calling and prepare ourselves for the task ahead.

Come, let us praise the Lord,
    for he is compassionate and long-suffering.
He hovers over us with an enduring love,
    and he girds us up in times of weakness.

Our God is a holy God,
        judging the earth in righteousness.
Our God is a just God,
        calling us to support the downtrodden.
Our God is a compassionate God,
        looking in mercy upon the poor and defenseless.
Our God is a majestic God,
        worthy of our praise and adoration.

INVOCATIONS

Leader: For this day of rest and worship,
People: WE PRAISE YOU, O GOD.
Leader: For your love revealed in Jesus Christ,
People: WE PRAISE YOU, O GOD.
Leader: For the meaning you have given to our lives,
People: WE PRAISE YOU, O GOD.
Leader: For your desire for justice and peace in our world,
People: WE PRAISE YOU, O GOD.

O God, be in our eyes,
    that we may perceive your being with understanding
    and view our neighbor's pain with sympathy.
O God, be in our heads,
    that we may comprehend your truth with clarity,
    and may evaluate ourselves with honesty.
O God, be in our mouths,
    that we may express our praise with joy,
    and may speak to others in kindness.
O God, be in our hearts,
    that we may endow our worship with sincerity,
    and may plan all our life with integrity.

Almighty God,
the Lord of the nations
and the hope of our battered world,
to whom else can we turn in these perilous times?
Hear our prayers for justice and peace,
and send your soothing Spirit
upon our troubled globe
and our anxious souls.

Receive, O Lord, our prayer of praise.
You are holiness; before you all evil trembles.
You are love; before you all hatred melts.
You are justice; before you all inequities are erased.
You are beauty; before you all ugliness vanishes.
You are truth; before you all falsehood slinks away.

We are disturbed and even frightened by the news we hear each day, and we praise you, God of Heaven, for your loving concern for all the people of your world. Help us, as your followers, to be part of the solution rather than part of the problem.

As we read the morning headlines and as we look around our country and our world, we become painfully aware that there is much which is not right. People are without homes, without jobs, without education, without basic human rights, without justice. Through your Word and Spirit move us to a new compassion, and prepare us to change our world.

PRAYERS OF CONFESSION

PRAYER OF CONFESSION

Leader: Let us come before the Lord, and in humility confess our failures to be truly Christian in our society.
For our silence in the face of injustice and discrimination,
People: FORGIVE US, WE PRAY.
Leader: For our willingness to take advantage of those who are poor and powerless,
People: FORGIVE US, WE PRAY.
Leader: For our spirit of discontent in the midst of comforts and luxuries,
People: FORGIVE US, WE PRAY.
Leader: For our reluctance to share our goods and ourselves with a desperately needy world,
People: FORGIVE US, WE PRAY, AND INSTILL WITHIN US THE SPIRIT OF JESUS, THE CHRIST.

WORDS OF ASSURANCE

We depend, not upon the justice of God, but upon his mercy; for while his justice must necessarily condemn, his mercy cannot help but forgive.

PRAYER OF CONFESSION

We confess, Lord,
that we have not always been the salt of the earth.
We have sometimes been so bland
that we meant nothing and changed nothing.
We have sometimes been so sharp
that people wondered whether we were really believers.
We have sometimes stayed so close to other Christians
that we had little opportunity to be the salt of our society.

Forgive us, Father, for our lack of distinctiveness and for our reluctance to invest ourselves in the common life of our community. Inspire us to a new willingness to lose ourselves for the sake of others.

WORDS OF ASSURANCE

Hear the good news: God is love, and those who draw on that love will be restored and renewed. Believe God's promises and receive God's pardon.

PRAYER OF CONFESSION

Leader: We confess, Father of humankind, that we have been nonchalant in a world of injustice.

People: WE HAVE SHRUGGED WHEN THE PLEASURE OF A FEW IS MADE POSSIBLE BY THE MISERY OF THE MANY.

Leader: We have done little when those without money were sentenced, and the rich walked out free.

People: WE HAVE BEEN SILENT AT THE SUPPRESSION OF THOSE WHO ARE OF THE WRONG COLOR, OR THE WRONG FAITH, OR THE WRONG SEX, OR THE WRONG NATIONALITY.

Leader: We have merely said "How awful" when we hear of increasing violence and bloodshed around the world.

People: WE HAVE SAID "THESE THINGS TAKE TIME" WHEN THE DISENFRANCHISED RAISE THEIR VOICES IN PROTEST.

Leader: Grant to us, Father of all, the compassion of him who wept over a stubborn city,

People: AND THE GODLY ANGER OF HIM WHO DROVE THE MONEYCHANGERS FROM THE TEMPLE.

WORDS OF ASSURANCE

The God who proclaims justice also offers mercy. Through the sacrifice of his Son, the Almighty has found a way to be both holy and kind, righteous and forgiving. Therefore we can come to him in confidence, knowing that he will pardon our waywardness and remember our sin no more.

PRAYER OF CONFESSION

Leader: If we have neglected the Lazaruses at our doorstep,
People: O GOD OF MERCY, FORGIVE.
Leader: If we have failed to defend the rights of the oppressed,
People: O GOD OF JUSTICE, FORGIVE.
Leader: If we have turned a deaf ear to cries of need,
People: O GOD OF COMPASSION, FORGIVE.
Leader: If we have remained silent about injustice in our world,
People: O GOD OF HOLINESS, FORGIVE.
Leader: If we have shrugged at the frustrations of those who are victims of prejudice,
People: O GOD OF ALL CREATION, FORGIVE.

WORDS OF ASSURANCE

Our Lord was anointed to preach good news to the poor,
to proclaim release to the captives,
to restore sight to the blind,
and to set at liberty the oppressed.

— Adapted from Luke 4:18

PRAYER OF CONFESSION

Forgive us, Father, for we have often ignored the social needs of our time.

We are no longer moved by pictures of the starving in Africa.

We drive past teeming apartments with little thought of the human tragedies taking place there.

We read the newspapers and shrug our shoulders.

We give a few dollars for relief, but do little to solve the problem.

We pass by on the other side, unwilling to become involved.

We would like to help, but don't know how we can find the time and energy.

Although we cannot do everything, help us to do something. Open our eyes to see the needs, and open our hands to meet those needs.

WORDS OF ASSURANCE

God sent the Son into the world, not to condemn the world, but that the world might be saved through him.

—John 3: 17

PRAYER OF CONFESSION

Leader: For neglecting the needs of our brothers and sisters
          until our own wants are fully satisfied,
People: FORGIVE US, CHRIST OF COMPASSION.
Leader: For making heroes of those who have attained wealth,
          power, and social status,
People: FORGIVE US, CHRIST OF SIMPLICITY.
Leader: For ignoring the needs of the disenfranchised by
          isolating ourselves from their neighborhoods and their
          needs,
People: FORGIVE US, CHRIST OF CONTINUING MERCY.
Leader: For glibly blaming the plight of others on character, race,
          or fate,
People: FORGIVE US, CHRIST OF UNIVERSAL ACCEPTANCE.

WORDS OF ASSURANCE

Jesus said, as he began his ministry:
"The Spirit of the Lord is on me,
because he has anointed me to preach good news to the poor.
He has sent me to proclaim freedom for the prisoners
and recovery of sight for the blind,
to release the oppressed,
to proclaim the year of the Lord's favor."

— Luke 4:18,19 (NIV)

PRAYER OF CONFESSION

Leader: For the times we have not loved God or our neighbors as we have loved ourselves,
People: LORD OF LOVE, FORGIVE US.
Leader: For the times we have passed by on the other side, pretending not to see the need,
People: LORD OF LOVE, FORGIVE US.
Leader: For the times we have said, "He should not have gotten himself into that situation,"
People: LORD OF LOVE, FORGIVE US.
Leader: For the times we have said, "Someone else will be along shortly to help,"
People: LORD OF LOVE, FORGIVE US.
Leader: For the times we neglected a person in pain as we hurried on to a religious duty,
People: LORD OF LOVE, FORGIVE US.

WORDS OF ASSURANCE

Let us live in love and bear one another's burdens, in the assurance that we are forgiven and are being made anew by the Spirit.

PRAYER OF CONFESSION

Leader: For the times we knowingly or unknowingly took advantage of the poor and powerless,

People: HEAR OUR PRAYER OF CONFESSION AND FORGIVE US BY YOUR GRACE.

Leader: For our hardness of heart in ignoring the plight of those who live in squalor,

People: HEAR OUR PRAYER OF CONFESSION AND FORGIVE US BY YOUR GRACE.

Leader: For the times we have made gods of money, prestige, and power,

People: HEAR OUR PRAYER OF CONFESSION AND FORGIVE US BY YOUR GRACE.

Leader: For the opportunities we have missed to be a positive force in bringing justice and relief for the poor,

People: HEAR OUR PRAYER OF CONFESSION AND FORGIVE US BY YOUR GRACE.

WORDS OF ASSURANCE

Blessed are those whose transgressions are forgiven,
whose sins are covered.
Blessed are those whose sin does not count against them
and in whose spirit is no deceit.

— Adapted from Psalm 32:1-2

PRAYER OF CONFESSION

Leader:	If we have turned a deaf ear to cries for help,
People:	PARDON AND ENCOURAGE US, MERCIFUL GOD.
Leader:	If we have not been true to the mind of Christ,
People:	FORGIVE AND STRENGTHEN US, HOLY GOD.
Leader:	If we have been blind to human suffering,
People:	FORGIVE AND SENSITIZE US, FAITHFUL GOD.
Leader:	If we have closed our hands in selfishness,
People:	PARDON AND CHANGE US, GENEROUS GOD.

WORDS OF ASSURANCE

Thus says the Lord:
Maintain justice, and do what is right,
for soon my salvation will come
and my deliverance be revealed.

—Isaiah 56:1

PRAYER OF CONFESSION

Leader:	From racism and prejudice; from the narrow-mindedness that fails to see the image of God in all people,
People:	GOOD LORD, DELIVER US.
Leader:	From arrogance and insensitivity; from the misplaced pride that demeans our brothers and sisters,
People:	GOOD LORD, DELIVER US.
Leader:	From injustice and greed; from the concentration of power that takes advantage of privilege,
People:	GOOD LORD, DELIVER US.
Leader:	From complacency and self-righteousness; from the salving of conscience by giving charity while denying basic rights,
People:	GOOD LORD, DELIVER US.

WORDS OF ASSURANCE

There is now therefore no condemnation for those who are in Christ Jesus. For the law of the Spirit of life in Christ Jesus has set you free from the law of sin and of death.

—Romans 8:1-2

GENERAL PRAYERS

LITANY OF INTERCESSION
(For those who have special needs)

Leader: For the wanderers, the rebellious, and the seekers,

People: WE CALL UPON YOUR SPIRIT.

Leader: For the abused and the abandoned, the helpless and the hopeless,

People: WE CALL UPON YOUR SPIRIT.

Leader: For the hospitalized and the immobilized, the painridden and the handicapped,

People: WE CALL UPON YOUR SPIRIT.

Leader: For the depressed and the anxious, the insecure and the confused,

People: WE CALL UPON YOUR SPIRIT.

Leader: For the homeless and the hungry, the disadvantaged and the unemployed,

People: WE CALL UPON YOUR SPIRIT.

Leader: For the refugees and the excluded, the exploited and the oppressed,

People: WE CALL UPON YOUR SPIRIT.

PRAYER OF INTERCESSION
(For those living in poverty)

As we sit here in the quietness of this sanctuary, we are keenly aware of the fact that there are many in our world like Lazarus in the parable of our Lord — people who are experiencing merciless poverty in the midst of affluence.

We confess that it is very easy for us to be judgmental toward those who have little. We feel better about it if we can blame poverty on such things as racial origin and personal laziness. We feel even better about it if we don't have to think about it at all.

Open our eyes to the injustices of our legal system, the inequities of our economic system, and the lethargy of our political system. Help us to be effective as we bring our Christian testimony to bear on all levels of government, in the market place, and in the courts. Help us to practice justice as individuals and to strive for justice as a corporate body. Help us to remember that as we have helped one of the least of our brethren, we have helped you.

PRAYER OF INTERCESSION
(For those In places of responsibility)

We pray for those in our society who have such places of responsibility and influence that they mightily affect the lives of thousands.

We pray for those whom have been chosen to represent us in the halls of government, whose laws affect the life and welfare of all of us, whose decisions can make war or peace, injustice or justice.

We pray for those who provide entertainment and those who are sports stars, who because of their fame are glorified as idols and role models.

We pray for those who write the books, the TV programs, the movies, and the plays which become part of our culture and national psyche.

We pray for those who are at the forefront of crusades and reforms, who are trying to raise our corporate consciousness concerning important issues of the day.

We pray for those who are spiritual leaders, to whom we turn for guidance in faith and ethics.

PRAYER OF PETITION
(For the victims of injustice)

We pray today for those of your children who are victims of injustice and tyranny:
—Those who because of the color of their skin are denied the right to vote, to live where they wish, or to decide their own destiny.
—Those who are held hostage, innocent pawns caught in the power struggle between nations.
—Those who have been brutalized and beaten by those who have taken vows to uphold and enforce the law.
—Those who are caught in a cycle of unemployment, poverty, ignorance, and despair.
—Those who languish in prisons for minor offenses, while others who have committed far greater crimes are set free because of wealth and influence.

PRAYER OF PETITION
(For our attitudes)

Realizing that we are sometimes negative in our thinking and critical in our opinion of others, we ask that you will heal our attitudes. Help us to greet each new day with anticipation, expecting the best. Remind us to try to understand others before condemning or criticizing them. Help us to be sensitive to the feelings of others, and not to look down on them because they have different likes and dislikes than we have. Help us to be open to suggestion and correction. May others detect in us the quiet hope of Christian confidence, and may they see in us a reflection of the compassion of Jesus Christ.

PRAYER OF PETITION
(For our attitude toward possessions)

God of love and God of wisdom, who provides for the birds of the air and for the animals of the field, we pray for greater wisdom in our attitude toward material things.

Free us, Lord, from the pressure to keep up with our neighbors; from the compulsion to buy things to impress others; from the foolishness of spending for things we really don't need and probably don't even want.

Give us the commitment to exercise Christian ethics in both the way we earn and the way we spend. In our earning may we not cheat others, and in our spending may we not deprive others of those things we ought to share.

Free us, Lord, from the anxiety which comes when we do not trust, and for the worry which comes when we close our eyes to your providential care. May we see clearly that life is more than clothing and that happiness is more than possessions.

PRAYER OF INTERCESSION
(For those who are poor)

As we sit in the comfort of this sanctuary, well dressed and well fed, we remember the millions in our world who will know nothing but poverty from the day they are born until the day they will die. Sustain them and make such adjustments in our fallen world as will enable them to live with dignity.

We pray for a sense of compassion and justice on the part of those who have vast holdings, but who pay their workers a starvation wage. We pray that governments may be sensitive to the needs of all of their people, and not just those who have economic and political clout.

We pray for rains in areas which have experienced severe drought, and we pray for those agencies which are bringing emergency help and long-term redevelopment.

We pray for young people who are struggling against tremendous odds to break the cycle of poverty, and we pray for those who are struggling with personal habits which are keeping them in a state of poverty and dependency.

PRAYER OF INTERCESSION
(For those who suffer hardship)

As we gather today in the comfort of this house of worship, we know that many today are suffering great hardship. So we pray for:
—children who are abused,
—spouses who are trapped in violent and unhappy relationships,
—refugees who have nowhere they can call home,
—people who live in cars and on the streets,
—those who are addicted to destructive drugs and destructive habits,
—the poor who must rely on public assistance in order to live,
—those who because of their faith are denied the right to a normal life and livelihood.

PRAYER OF PETITION
(For our daily work)

We are grateful for being able to work—for keenness of mind, for strength of muscle, and for the dexterity which coordinates the two. We give thanks for the ability to learn new tasks, to cope with difficult situations, to adjust to the changing technology of our day. We are thankful for the opportunity of this great land and for the system which encourages individual effort and self-esteem.

We pray for justice in the world of work. May there be equal pay for equal work; may there be fairness in hiring; and may there be equality of opportunity for advancement.

Bless all of us in our daily work. May we be honest in our dealings, responsible in our investments, and fair in all our relationships. May we see all of our tasks in their sacred dimension—in relation to you as well as to each other.

PRAYER OF THANKS AND INTERCESSION
(For those who work)

We thank you for the privilege of work— for the strength of body and clarity of mind that make it possible to earn a living. We are grateful also for the fulfillment that our work gives us—not only the satisfaction of supporting ourselves and our families, but also the satisfaction of meeting the challenges that each workday brings.

At the same time, we raise a sympathetic prayer for those who dislike their work. Open new doors and new opportunities for them, either within their present jobs or outside of them. Help them to maintain a good relationship with others and to have a good attitude.

We pray, also, for those who, despite their best efforts, cannot find work. Help them to maintain a positive self image, even though it is difficult under the circumstances. Give them persistence and patience, and lead them to the fulfillment of self-support.

PRAYER OF INTERCESSION
(For government leaders)

Ruler of all nations. we pray for government leaders around the world. It fills us with both hope and fear to realize that the health, freedom, and welfare of millions of people rests in the hands of a few key people.

Even if they may not specifically honor and serve you, may these leaders live and rule by the principles which have their origin in you — the principles of justice, love, mercy, and wisdom.

Replace distrust and suspicion with mutual respect. Replace ancient hatreds and hostilities with a new sympathy for one another's humanity. Help political leaders everywhere to place a higher priority on the welfare of their people than on the prestige and power of their own careers.

OFFERTORY SENTENCES

Since there will never cease to be some in need on the earth, I therefore command you, "Open your hand to the poor and needy neighbor in your land."

—Deuteronomy 15:11

Whoever is kind to the poor lends to the Lord, and will be repaid in full.

—Proverbs 19:17

If you close your ear to the cry of the poor, you will cry out and not be heard.

—Proverbs 21:13

Whatever you wish that others would do to you, do so to them, for this is the law and the prophets.

—Matthew 7: 12

Jesus said to his disciples, "If any want to become my followers, let them deny themselves and take up their cross and follow me."

—Matthew 16:24

Truly I tell you, just as you did it to one of the least of these who are members of my family, you did it to me.

—Matthew 25:40

As we give, let us remember the haunting question of Christ, "Which of these three, do you think, proved neighbor to the man who fell among the robbers?"

—Luke 10:36

As we give, we follow the example of the Christians in Antioch, who, in proportion to their ability, sent relief to their fellow believers in Judea — sending it to the elders of the church by the hand of Barnabas and Paul.

—Adapted from Acts 11:29-30

Let each of you look not to your own interests, but to the interests of others.
—Philippians 2:4

Those who desire to be rich fall into temptation, into a snare, into many senseless and hurtful desires that plunge people into ruin and destruction. For the love of money is the root of all evils; it is through this craving that some have wandered from the faith and pierced their hearts with many pangs.
—1 Timothy 6:9-10

What good is it, my brothers and sisters, if you say you have faith but do not have works? Can faith save you? If a brother or sister is naked and lacks daily food, and one of you says to them, "Go in peace; keep warm and eat your fill," and yet you do not supply their bodily needs, what is the good of that? So faith by itself, if it has no works, is dead.
—James 2:14-17

How does God's love abide in anyone who has the world's goods and sees a brother or sister in need and yet refuses help? Little children, let us love, not in word or speech, but in truth and action.
—1 John 3:17-18

Through our generous offerings, let us express our two-fold love: love for God and love for others.

As we give, let us remember our high privilege to be salt and light, to make a real impact on a world which desperately needs our Christian witness.

OFFERTORY PRAYERS

Thank you, Father, for our daily work —
for the skills you have given us,
for the health we have enjoyed,
for the positive contribution we make to our common life,
for the paychecks which supply our needs,
and for the added privilege of giving some of our bounty for the welfare of our world and the sharing of your love.

We ask, Father, that you will bless not only that which we give, but also that which we retain.
That larger portion — which we use for our family, our pleasure, and our business — is also a divine trust. May we use it with honesty, integrity, and good judgment.

We are thankful, Father, not only for the good things we receive, but also for the good things we can give. It gives us satisfaction to know that our offerings will be translated into literature for Christian education, food for the hungry, medical care for the sick, bricks and mortar for church buildings, pastoral care for your people, and a hundred other services which will bring help, light, and peace.

We give these offerings as an act of love.
We give in love for our families and other families
    who look to the church for spiritual guidance.
We give in love for the people of the world
    who are victims of injustice, war, and natural calamity,
    who look to the church for assistance.
We give in love for the citizens of our planet
    who are without hope and spiritual direction,
    who look to the church for the good news of God's grace.

We thank you, Lord, for our possessions — for the confidence they give us, for the enjoyment they produce, and for the freedom they make possible. We also thank you for one additional blessing — the privilege of sharing with others and of investing in a cause larger than ourselves.

We ask that through these offerings the church will be empowered to do your will: to proclaim your word, to extend your invitation of healing and new life, to aid the poor, and to be a transforming power in your world.

It is our prayer that these gifts will make a difference; that because of our generosity lives will be changed, souls will be saved, bodies will be fed, living conditions will be improved, and minds will be enlightened.

With these gifts we declare that we are free from the slavery to things, and that we wish our lives to be regulated by the standards of Jesus Christ rather than by the standards of our society.

Help us to realize that our citizenship is dual — that we have privileges and obligations to our nation here, but that our ultimate allegiance is to your sovereign rule, which is universal.

Help us, Lord Jesus, to express through these gifts our message to the world: a message of mercy, a message of justice, a message of love, a message of peace.

As we give, we remember James' statement that "faith by itself, if it has no works, is dead" (James 2:17). May our works exhibit the presence of true faith; and may our faith validate itself by a transformed life.

Leader: For the strengthening of the church,
People: WE PRESENT THESE GIFTS.
Leader: As an expression of God's love,
People: WE PRESENT THESE GIFTS.
Leader: In the cause of justice and peace,
People: WE PRESENT THESE GIFTS.

BENEDICTIONS

In the market place, in the school, in the factory, and in the home, live in such a way that justice will roll down like waters, and righteousness like an ever-flowing stream.
—Inspired by Amos 5:24

As individuals, as families,
and as citizens of this land,
heed the words of the prophet Amos,
"Let justice roll down like waters,
and righteousness like an everflowing stream"
— Amos 5:24

The Spirit of the Lord is upon you,
sending you, as he sent Christ,
to share the gospel with the poor,
to heal the brokenhearted,
to preach deliverance to those who are bound,
to give sight to the blind,
to set at liberty those who are oppressed,
and to proclaim that this is the acceptable year of the Lord.
—Adapted from Luke 4:18-19

Beloved, let us love one another,
for love is of God,
and those who love are born of God and know God.
—Adapted from 1 John 4:7

Abound, more and more,
in love,
in justice,
in knowledge, and in wisdom,
for God is at work in you
bringing forth the fruits of the Spirit.

May your faith be translated into life,
your convictions be expressed in actions,
your words become incarnate in deeds;
and may you do all through the power of God's Spirit.

Return tomorrow to your daily tasks,
enjoying strength of body and keenness of mind,
finding satisfaction in your work
and good relationships with fellow laborers.
May you be honest in all your dealings,
and may you do all to the glory of God.

May your faith bring peace.
May your victories bring joy.
May your difficulties bring growth.
May your service bring satisfaction.
And may the grace of God be with you always.

Live at peace with all.
Share with others the compassion of Christ.
Recognize the needs of those around you.
Open your hands to the poor.

Support the weak.
Work for that which is fair and just.
Defend the oppressed.
Encourage one another in the Lord.

Be the salt of the earth;
permeating,
preserving,
purifying.

CALLS TO WORSHIP

Now, in Jesus,
we who used to be at a distance
have been brought very close,
for he has broken down the barriers
which formerly kept us apart.
He has erased the hostility among us
and has brought us the good news of peace.
—Adapted from Ephesians 2:13-17

We worship the Christ who is the image of the invisible God,
the head of the body, the church,
the first born from among the dead,
the one who has reconciled all things to himself,
who made peace by the blood of the cross.
—Adapted from Colossians 1:15-20

As we wait with anticipation
for the visit or letter from a friend,
for the voice of a loved one on the phone,
for the breaking of day after a dark and lonely night,
so let us wait for the Lord,
straining to hear the sound of his voice,
eager to feel the stirrings of the Spirit,
and longing to experience the joy of his presence.

Leader: Our help is in the name of the Lord, who made heaven
          and earth.
People: GREAT IS THE LORD AND WORTHY OF ALL
          PRAISE.
Leader: God so loved the world that he gave his only son.
People: GREAT IS THE LORD AND WORTHY OF ALL
          PRAISE.
Leader: Christ is our peace, for he has broken down our walls of
          hostility.
People: GREAT IS THE LORD AND WORTHY OF ALL
          PRAISE.

Come, let us lift up our voices
  to sing the praises of the Lord.
Come, let us lift up our spirits
  to seek his will for our lives.
Come, let us stretch out our hands,
  and welcome all people to his family.

He who prayed that all who believe may be one,
who has broken down the walls of hostility,
calls us to worship
united by our common Savior,
united by the Holy Spirit,
and united by love.

Come, brothers and sisters in the faith,
let us gather with the God who cares for us as a father,
who comforts us as a mother,
who walks with us as a brother or sister,
and who listens to us as a friend.

"And people shall come from the east and west, and from north and south," prophesied Jesus, "and shall sit at table in the kingdom of God" (Luke 13:29).
We are already a partial fulfillment of that prophecy, for we represent many nationalities; and we come from many states and countries; and among us are many diversities of wealth, custom, and religious roots.
Yet we are gathered at one table, and we gather at the invitation of one host, and we share one faith, one Spirit, one baptism, and one hope of eternal life.

Leader: Let us come together in love,
People: LOVING GOD AND LOVING EACH OTHER FOR GOD'S SAKE.
Leader: Let us come together in peace,
People: FOR GOD HAS BROKEN DOWN THE WALLS THAT DIVIDE US.
Leader: Let us come together in hope,
People: KNOWING THAT WE ARE SECURE IN GOD, WHO HAS SAVED US.

Leader: God's mercy is a very wide mercy,
People: ENCIRCLING ALL THE PEOPLE WHO LIVE UPON
          THE EARTH.
Leader: God's mercy is a very deep mercy,
People: REACHING TO THE DEPTHS OF THE HUMAN SOUL.
Leader: God's mercy is a very high mercy,
People: LIFTING US TO HEIGHTS OF FREEDOM AND
          ACCOMPLISHMENT.

Peace

INVOCATIONS

As we gather to worship today, we pray for our brothers and sisters around the world who have also come to honor the Christ. Some have gathered in huge cathedrals, and others have gathered in jungle clearings. Some are gathered in country churches, and others have come together in storefront churches. Some are worshipping in churches of brick, others in churches of wood, and still others in churches of mud and thatch.

Whoever your people are, and whatever their color and language, we ask that you will bless them as they gather to worship.

Out of all peoples in the world you have called us to be your church, your flock, your nation, your people, Jew and Gentile, black and white, rich and poor, old and young. Bless, now, all who have answered your call, and fill them with your goodness and glory.

Leader: In our worship, in our breaking of bread together, in our singing as a single voice,
People: BY YOUR SPIRIT MAKE US ONE.
Leader: In our faithfulness to each other and to our Lord and Savior Jesus Christ,
People: BY YOUR SPIRIT MAKE US ONE.
Leader: In our concern for others and in our commitment to serve our world,
People: BY YOUR SPIRIT MAKE US ONE.

It is a beautiful day, Lord, not just because of the weather outside or the wonders of your creation. It is beautiful because of the climate of love and peace that pervades our souls because of your Spirit's presence. Open our eyes and our hearts, that we may fully appreciate all the true beauty of this day.

130

Grant us, Lord, the perception to tell the difference between the transient and the eternal.

Enable us to distinguish between the truths of God which unite us and the traditions of people which divide us.

Concerning the transient, give us a spirit of conciliatory grace.

Concerning the eternal, give us a spirit of dedicated conviction.

And in all, give us a spirit of love.

As we gather in this house of worship,
challenge us, O God, with your truth
and inspire us with your love.
Then as we return to our worlds of work and learning and living,
enlighten us with your wisdom
and empower us with your strength.

We remember the promise of Jesus that "Where two or three are gathered in my name, there am I in the midst of them" (Matt. 18:20). We are more than two or three, we are gathered in your name, and we are confident of your presence among us. Consecrate our association with each other and with Christ, and bind us together in Christian love.

You know, Lord, that in our world there is so much unrest, so much crime, so much anger, so many wars, so much anxiety. Help us, in the quietness of this hour, to experience the deep peace that can come only from you.

But we come, not to escape the realities of our world, but to receive the strength to deal with them. Help us not only to experience peace, but also to create it. Enable us not only to be peace receivers but also to become peace makers.

PRAYERS OF CONFESSION

PRAYER OF CONFESSION

God of all the earth,
whose Son prayed that his followers would become one,
forgive our divisiveness.
We confess that we are often critical of people who believe
    differently than we do,
that we sometimes lack charity toward those whose customs are
    different,
that our humor is sometimes based on ethnic slurs,
and that we have placed a low priority on peacemaking.
Forgive the arrogance that claims all truth,
the pride that closes ears to others,
and the insensitivity that disregards hurt feelings.
Heal our broken fellowship in your mercy,
and make us truly unified as the children of one God.

WORDS OF ASSURANCE

There is neither Jew nor Gentile, black nor white,
there is neither slave nor free, rich nor poor,
there is neither male nor female, young nor old,
for all of us are one in Christ.

PRAYER OF CONFESSION

Leader: Hear us, O Lord, as we confess our divisions.
People: INCLINE YOUR EAR AS WE SHARE OUR WEAKNESS.
Leader: We are created to serve one Lord,
People: BUT WE FOLLOW MANY MASTERS.
Leader: We are called to be one people,
People: BUT WE OFTEN GRUMBLE ABOUT EACH OTHER.
Leader: We are to confess one faith and one baptism,
People: BUT WE REWRITE OUR CREEDS WITH INCREAS-
         ING DIVISIVENESS.
Leader: We are called to be peacemakers,
People: BUT WE MORE OFTEN HAVE BEEN CONTENTIOUS.
Leader: Help us, Lord, to accept one another with civility and
         grace,
People: FOR YOU HAVE CALLED US TO BOW TOGETHER
         AT THE FOOT OF THE CROSS.

WORDS OF ASSURANCE

The God who reconciled us to himself will also help us to be
reconciled to each other. The one who broke down the barriers
between himself and humankind will also break down the barriers
which we have created among ourselves.

PRAYER OF CONFESSION

Leader: That we may understand clearly where we have been
          disobedient and rebellious in our relationship with the
          King of Kings,
People: WE WILL PRAY TO THE LORD AND SEEK
          FORGIVENESS.
Leader: That we may acknowledge without excuse our own
          responsibility for the unhappy tangle of human
          relationships.
People: WE WILL PRAY TO THE LORD AND ASK FOR
          PARDON.
Leader: That we may recognize the changes that should take
          place in our lives,
People: WE WILL PRAY TO THE LORD AND SEEK DIVINE
          STRENGTH.

WORDS OF ASSURANCE

Brothers and sisters in Christ,
you are cleansed from sin,
you are forgiven in Christ,
you are citizens of a new kingdom —
a kingdom of peace and justice
which will never come to an end.

PRAYER OF CONFESSION

Leader: Forgive, Lord, our failures in Christian love.
People: WE FIND IT EASY TO LOVE THOSE WHO LOVE US, AND EASY TO DISLIKE THOSE WHO DISLIKE US.
Leader: We appreciate those who think as we do, but we are critical of those who disagree.
People: WE ARE ATTRACTED TO THOSE WHO ARE SIMILAR TO US, BUT WE FEEL UNCOMFORTABLE WITH THOSE WHO ARE DIFFERENT.
Leader: We allow differences in class, color, and creed to become barriers between us.
People: WE EXPRESS APPRECIATION ONLY WHEN WE FEEL WE HAVE SOMETHING TO GAIN.
Leader: We withdraw from others because we don't want to risk rejection.
People: FOR THESE SINS AGAINST THE MOST BEAUTIFUL OF HUMAN BONDS, WE ASK FORGIVENESS, IN THE NAME OF HIM WHO — EVEN WHEN WE WERE ENEMIES — LOVED US AND GAVE HIMSELF FOR US.

WORDS OF ASSURANCE

Leader: No longer enemies, we are friends of God.
People: NO LONGER WANDERERS, WE HAVE FOUND A HOME.
Leader: No longer strangers, we love and are loved.
People: NO LONGER ORPHANS, WE ARE THE CHILDREN OF GOD.

135

PRAYER OF CONFESSION

How often, Father, have we not prayed for your kingdom's coming,
yet have barred others from it.
We have felt uncomfortable in the presence of "outsiders."
We have built our own empires.
We have failed to answer the call to service.
We have been unconcerned about our divisions.
We have given only modestly to your kingdom's support.
We have neglected its extension around the world.
Enable us, our Father, to substantiate our prayers with deeds,
and to seek first your kingdom and your righteousness
in faith that the rest will come to us in due time.

WORDS OF ASSURANCE

The Lord is just in all his ways,
and kind in all his doings.
The Lord is near to all who call upon him,
to all who call upon him in truth.

—Psalm 145:17-18

PRAYER OF CONFESSION

O God of kindness and harmony, we are dismayed that while we honor the Prince of Peace our world is agonized by war, violence, and anger. Christ came to reconcile us with you and with each other, but we human beings have continued to rebel against you and to wage war with each other.

Forgive, Lord, our personal and corporate guilt. Some of us are at odds with each other; most of us harbor prejudices and animosities; some of us have caused problems in the church, in the home, and in our social groups; and most of us have failed to take an active role in the pursuit of global peace. Show us how to become peacemakers, both as individuals and as members of the worldwide fellowship of humankind.

WORDS OF ASSURANCE

"Blessed are the peacemakers," said Jesus, "for they will be called children of God."

— Matthew 5:9

PRAYER OF CONFESSION

Leader: Reach across the barriers that divide nationality from nationality and race from race.

People: RECONCILE US, O CHRIST, BY YOUR CRADLE AND CROSS.

Leader: Reach across the barriers that divide men from women, young from old, rich from poor.

People: RECONCILE US, O CHRIST, BY YOUR CRADLE AND CROSS.

Leader: Reach across the barriers that divide Christian from Christian.

People: RECONCILE US, O CHRIST, BY YOUR CRADLE AND CROSS.

Leader: Reach across the barriers that divide us from our families and neighbors.

People: RECONCILE US, O CHRIST, BY YOUR CRADLE AND CROSS.

WORDS OF ASSURANCE

"I have other sheep that are not of this sheep pen," said Jesus. "I must bring them also. They too will listen to my voice, and there shall be one flock and one shepherd."

— John 10:16, NIV

PRAYER OF CONFESSION

There is much injustice in the world, Lord,
but we are not sure what we can do about it.
There is much discrimination,
and we wonder how we can even begin to help.
There is much prejudice,
and we know that the patterns are deep set in tradition.
We also know that we have sometimes been part of the problem
rather than part of the solution,
and that we have been content to stand idly by
when we should have been dedicated and involved.
Forgive us, Lord, for our complicity and our complacency,
and give us the spirit of the Master,
who invited himself to the home of a Publican,
fully accepting an outcast of his society.

WORDS OF ASSURANCE

In Christ God was reconciling the world to himself, not counting
their trespasses against them, and entrusting to us the message of
reconciliation.

—2 Corinthians 5:19

PRAYER OF CONFESSION

Forgive us, Lord, for the sins we have committed even as we
have gathered here.

Pardon us, we pray, for wandering minds and inattentive hearts.

Forgive us for concentrating more on the clothing of others than
upon the word of faith.

Deliver us from smoldering jealousy and from animosity hidden
behind congeniality.

Forgive us for dragging into your holy house the resentments,
the hurts, and the anger of the week past.

Remove, Lord, the sins of this hour, and by so doing purify us for
the hours of the week to come.

WORDS OF ASSURANCE

Now the Lord is the Spirit, and where the Spirit of the Lord is, there
is freedom.

— 2 Corinthians 3:17

PRAYER OF CONFESSION

Leader: Forgive us, Lord of love, for being insensitive and unloving.
People: FOR CUTTING DOWN OUR LOVED ONES IN PRIVATE AND EVEN IN PUBLIC.
Leader: For hurting the reputations of others with subtle innuendos.
People: FOR MIMICKING PEOPLE OF OTHER NATIONALITIES AND RACES.
Leader: For being insensitive in our remarks to the handicapped.
People: FOR SHRUGGING OFF THE PROBLEMS OF OTHERS AS BEING OF NO CONCERN TO US.
Leader: Forgive us, Lord,
People: AND PATTERN OUR MINDS AFTER THE MIND OF CHRIST.

WORDS OF ASSURANCE

Leader: God destined us in love to be his children through Jesus Christ.
People: IN HIM WE HAVE REDEMPTION THROUGH HIS BLOOD, THE FORGIVENESS OF OUR TRESPASSES, ACCORDING TO THE RICHES OF HIS GRACE WHICH HE LAVISHED UPON US.
                              —Adapted from Ephesians 1:7-8

PRAYER OF CONFESSION

We come, O God of all people everywhere, confessing that our attitudes and actions have separated us from you and from each other. When we hear other accents, we are sometimes amused and sometimes annoyed. When we see people of other shades and colors, we make judgments based on appearance. When we encounter varying expressions and emphases of faith, we are suspicious. Forgive us, God, and renew within us a spirit of compassion and understanding. Give us the gift of humility, and fill us with the vision of unity in Christ.

WORDS OF ASSURANCE

Glory be to Christ, by whose blood God has ransomed his people from every tribe, tongue, and nation, and has made them a kingdom and priests to serve God, and they will reign on earth.
— Adapted from Revelation 5:9-10

GENERAL PRAYERS

PRAYER OF PETITION
(For peace)

Although we celebrate the gathering of Jew and Gentile at the manger of the Christ-child, we are painfully aware that this unity is not a reality in our world today. We pray that all people everywhere may have a hunger and thirst for peace, and that the name of Jesus may be a unifying rather than divisive factor in our world.

We hang our heads in shame when we remember the religious and racial animosity between Jew and Gentile, Arab and Jew, Protestant and Catholic, liberal and conservative, black and white, and between all those other divisions which we are so eager to make among ourselves. No matter what our personal convictions, give us the grace to seek peace and harmony among all who are members of the human family.

PRAYER OF INTERCESSION
(For peace in our time)

We are bold to pray that peace may come to our hostile and troubled world. We pray that dividing walls may crumble and that those who have been alienated may reach across with open hands.

May suspicions be replaced by trust. May hatreds be replaced by tolerance. May those who have refused to talk sit down and express their common concerns. May negotiations become the alternative to armed conflict, and may reasonable people sit down and reason together.

We pray especially for the persons and movements which are trying to eliminate the root causes of war — inequality, injustice, and discrimination. May there be justice in our land and around the world, and may we respect each other's sacred rights. May freedom ring, and may power be used to heal instead of to alienate.

141

PRAYER OF THANKSGIVING
(For peacemakers)

As we honor the one whose birth was announced as an event of peace and good will, we raise our prayer of thanks for those who have invested themselves in the quest for peace.

We are grateful for presidents, for prime ministers, and — yes — even for dictators who have committed themselves to making our world a place of peace and security. We are grateful that some of our world leaders are willing to place the welfare of our globe as a greater priority than national prestige.

We are thankful for those who negotiate secretly behind the scenes; who without receiving credit or recognition are trying to bring together stubborn and selfish national leaders to the point of compromise and civility.

We are grateful for those in our own church and community who exert a calming effect upon the unhappy situations and tensions of our life together. May people outside the church see in Christians a living proof that Christ's kingdom of peace is indeed already here.

PRAYER OF PRAISE
(For the rich diversity of people in the world)

We raise our prayers of praise for the infinite variety of your creation, for the wide diversity of people whom you have placed in our world, and for the rich heritage we can share with each other as children of the same God.

We praise you for shades of skin color and for variety of facial features. We praise you for the diversity of ethnic foods we can enjoy, and even more than that we thank you for the privilege of sitting down together at the banquet table of our Lord.

It is our prayer that our differences may enrich rather than divide, and that our diversity may bring respect rather than derision. Help us never to despise another person because of race, creed, color, or gender. Give us, instead, a keen appreciation for the varieties of human nature and culture which make our world such an interesting place to live.

PRAYER OF THANKS
(For the contributions of many cultures)

God of all nations, who has created the people of our earth in an incredible variety of colors, cultures, and creeds, we are grateful for the contributions which many have made to our common life.

Some have taught us to live at peace with the environment; others have taught us the importance of eliminating bigotry and discrimination. Some have taught us about excellence in work; and others have set for us an example of family care and solidarity. All have enriched us with their music, their food, their clothing, their customs, their language, their convictions, and their heritage. Thank you, O God of all peoples everywhere, for the enrichment of our lives through the diversity of your children.

PRAYER OF INTERCESSION
(For those who suffer for being different)

We raise our prayers of petition for those who suffer by the hand of other human beings simply because they are different.

We pray for the poor, who because they do not have financial clout cannot receive justice in a court of law, and who are taken advantage of by the rich.

We pray for those who, when they attend church are not warmly received because they are poorly dressed, or are of the wrong nationality or race or social status.

We pray for the handicapped, who often are the object of stares and of thoughtless remarks, and who are denied access to many public facilities, and who are not recognized for their gifts.

We pray for those whose color of skin becomes the criteria for hiring, for friendships, for education, for promotion, and for housing.

We pray for those who are denied public or religious office, or equal pay, or equal advancement, because they are women.

PRAYER OF INTERCESSION
(For those who are Instruments of change)

With a mixture of admiration and uncertainty we pray for those who are seeking to bring about change in our world.

We pray for the revolutionaries in our society, that their motives may be pure, that their objectives may be worthy, and that their methods will never include violence and the destruction of human life.

We pray for those who have committed themselves to peaceful change, who are seeking legislation which will protect human life at every stage, who are advancing unpopular but worthy causes.

We pray for our fellow citizens who are trying to change public opinion, who are taking issue with commonly-held assumptions and traditions, who are facing formidable opposition from well-organized and well-financed special interest groups.

PRAYER OF PETITION
(That we may learn to love)

O God, you are the fountain of love and the author of the command to love. Therefore we ask you to teach us to love.

Teach us to love even when our love is not returned, and even when our love is spurned. Make us confident that in its own time and in its own place love will bring a response.

Teach us to love even when the object of that love seems unworthy of love, and when we love only by making up our mind to do so.

Teach us to love when it would be easier to hate; teach us to love when it would be easier to ignore; teach us to love when it would be easier to leave.

Teach us to love even when our love has been betrayed, when only forgiveness will make love possible, when only grace will keep love alive, when only patience will see love bloom.

OFFERTORY SENTENCES

So when you are offering your gift at the altar, if you remember that your brother or sister has something against you, leave your gift there before the altar and go; first be reconciled to your brother or sister, and then come and offer your gift.
—Matthew 5:23, 24

Fear not, little flock, for it is your Father's good pleasure to give you the kingdom. Sell your possessions, and give alms; provide yourselves with purses that do not grow old, with a treasure in the heavens that does not fail, where no thief approaches and no moth destroys. For where your treasure is, there will your heart be also.
— Luke 12:32-34

If we give away all we have, and even if we deliver our bodies to be burned, but do so without love, we have gained nothing.
— Adapted from 1 Corinthians 13:3

So then, as we have opportunity, let us do good to all people, especially to those who are of the household of faith.
— Adapted from Galatians 6:10

We know that we have passed from death to life because we love one another.
— 1 John 3:14

God does not want us to be holding tanks,
forever receiving, never being satisfied,
always wanting more, keeping everything for ourselves.
Rather, God wishes us to be pipelines,
conduits of his mercy, instruments of his grace,
giving as well as receiving, sharing as well as keeping.

As our Lord's earthly ministry touched many who were outside the generally-accepted household of faith, so these gifts will also reach far beyond us: to those of different colors, cultures, and creeds. Following the example and spirit of our Lord, let us give generously.

Through our gifts we can become reconcilers and peacemakers in a troubled, selfish, and often hate-filled world. May our prayers and our personal efforts accompany our financial gifts so we can become positive forces for love and understanding.

OFFERTORY PRAYERS

As we give, may we have a sense of being co-workers with you in the greatest task on earth — that of bringing peace, life, and meaning to our fellow human beings.

In presenting this offering we are accepting the invitation of Paul when he said, "Therefore as we have opportunity, let us do good to all people, especially to those who belong to the family of believers" (Gal. 6:10, NIV). Some of these gifts are for the family of believers, and others are for the greater family of humankind, but all of these gifts are given in gratitude to you, the Father of us all.

We remember the words of the Apostle, who said that we will glorify God by the generosity of our contribution (2 Cor. 9:13). May your name now be glorified as we generously share these gifts.

We approach you, Lord, as one who can take common things and common people, consecrate them by your love, and make them holy. We ask you now to do just that with these, our gifts.

We ask, O Creator of all people everywhere,
that you will use these gifts to break down barriers:
the barriers of race, the barriers of culture,
the barriers of economics, the barriers of faith,
until we all become one through the miracle of your love.

Leader: Because we honor our Sovereign,
People: WE GIVE THESE OFFERINGS.
Leader: Because we see neighbors in need,
People: WE PRESENT THESE GIFTS.
Leader: Because we believe in the mission of the church,
People: WE DEDICATE THESE OFFERINGS.

We rejoice, O God, in the time and talents you have given us, gifts that enable us both to earn a living and to share with others. Bless that which we keep and multiply that which we give, for both come from you.

Leader: Because we wish to be wise in the use of our possessions,
People: WE INVEST THESE GIFTS IN THE WORK OF YOUR CHURCH.
Leader: Because we are grateful for the material and spiritual resources you have given us,
People: WE RETURN A PORTION TO YOU, OUR GRACIOUS GOD.

We celebrate the world-wide significance of our gifts — gifts which cut across barriers of culture and creed; gifts which make insignificant the differences of race and language; gifts which bind us together in a fellowship of caring and hope.

Help us, O God,
to enlarge the circle of our concern.
May that circle include not only ourselves, our friends, and our families,
but people around the world whom we do not know,
also created in your image.

Already, in your divine wisdom, you know those whose lives will be touched by our gifts. Bless those people, whoever they are and wherever they live, and use these gifts to convey the healing and transforming power of Jesus Christ.

Leader: Because we who have freely received are challenged to freely give,
People: WE PRESENT THESE GIFTS.
Leader: Because we have been blessed in order to be a blessing .
People: WE PRESENT THESE GIFTS.
Leader: Because we who have been loved are inspired to love others.
People: WE PRESENT THESE GIFTS.

BENEDICTIONS

If it is possible, so far as it depends on you, live peaceably with all.
—Romans 12:18

Do not be overcome by evil, but overcome evil with good.
—Romans 12:21

Agree with one another,
live in peace,
and the God of love and peace will be with you.
—2 Corinthians 13:11b

Leader: This service is over, but our witness as Christians goes on.
People: WE PLEDGE TO LEAD A LIFE WORTHY OF OUR CALLING, WITH ALL HUMILITY, GENTLENESS, AND PATIENCE, FORBEARING ONE ANOTHER IN LOVE.
Leader: Go, then, to your homes, keeping the unity of the Spirit in the bond of peace.
—Adapted from Ephesians 4:1-3

Become instruments of God's noble purpose,
cleansed and made holy,
prepared for every good work.
—Adapted from 2 Timothy 2:21

Become a neighbor to all,
weeping with those who weep,
rejoicing with those who rejoice,
befriending those who are lonely,
and helping those who are in need.

May dividing walls crumble.
May suspicions disappear and hatreds cease.
May your divisions be healed,
and may you live in justice and peace.

Become instruments of God's peace.
Where there is hatred, sow love.
Where there is injury, pardon.
Where there is doubt, faith.
Where there is despair, hope.
Where there is darkness, light.
Where there is sadness, joy.
   —Adapted from a prayer by St. Francis of Assisi, 1181-1226

Go from this place and be at peace,
at peace with God, for Christ has reconciled you;
at peace with others, because love is the essence of the Law;
at peace with yourself, for you embody God's image.

You who have received God's peace
and have been reconciled by the blood of Christ
and now commissioned to be signs and sources of peace
in a hostile and hurting world.

Become instruments of God's peace —
at peace with your God,
at peace with your brothers and sisters, God's children,
and at peace with yourself, created in God's image.

Go to your homes,
remembering that you are loved
and that you are to love one another
as God in Christ has loved you.

May the Lord bless and keep us all:
men and women, young and old,
newcomer and long-time member,
rich and poor, black and brown and white,
conservative and liberal.
May God give us all a sense of community,
and may we live in peace and understanding.

CALLS TO WORSHIP

God saw everything that he had made, and indeed, it was very good. ...Thus the heavens and the earth were finished, and all their multitude. And on the seventh day God finished the work he had done, and he rested on the seventh day from all the work he had done. So God blessed the seventh day and hallowed it.

—Genesis 1:31 to 2:3

Let the sea roar, and all that fills it;
the world and those who live in it.
Let the floods clap their hands;
let the hills sing together for joy
at the presence of the Lord,
for he is coming to judge the earth.
He will judge the world with righteousness,
and the peoples with equity.

—Psalm 98:7-9

Bless the Lord, O my soul.
O Lord my God, you are very great.
You are clothed with honor and majesty,
wrapped in light as with a garment.
You stretch out the heavens like a tent,
you set the beams of your chambers on the waters,
you make the clouds your chariot,
you ride on the wings of the wind,
you make the winds your messengers,
fire and flame are your ministers.
Bless the Lord, O my soul.
Praise the Lord!

— Psalm 104:1-4, 35b*

*The entire Psalm 104 is on the subject of God as creator and provider.

Leader: We will seek the Lord and his strength!
People: WE WILL SEEK HIS PRESENCE CONTINUALLY!
Leader: We will remember the wonderful works he has done!
People: WE WILL REMEMBER HIS MIRACLES AND THE
          TEACHINGS HE HAS UTTERED!
                              —Adapted from Psalm 105:4-5

Leader: Let us thank God for his steadfast love,
People: FOR HIS WONDERFUL WORKS AMONG HUMANKIND.
Leader: Let us extol God in the congregation of the people,
People: AND PRAISE HIM IN THE ASSEMBLY OF BELIEVERS.
                              —Adapted from Psalm 107:31-32

Leader: Praise, O servants of the Lord, praise the name of the
          Lord!
People: BLESSED BE THE NAME OF THE LORD FROM THIS
          TIME FORTH AND FOR EVER MORE.
Leader: From the rising of the sun to its setting, the name of the
          Lord is to be praised!
People: THE LORD IS HIGH ABOVE ALL NATIONS, AND HIS
          GLORY ABOVE THE HEAVENS.
                              —Psalm 113:1-4

Praise the Lord!
Praise the Lord from the heavens,
praise him in the heights!
Praise him, all his angels,
praise him, all his host!
Praise him, sun and moon,
praise him, all you shining stars!
Praise him, you highest heavens,
and you waters above the heavens!
Praise the Lord!

                              — Psalm 148:1-4, 146

Holy, holy, holy is the Lord of hosts;
the whole earth is full of his glory.

—Isaiah 6:3

Leader: How great are God's signs!
People: HOW GREAT ARE GOD'S WONDERS!
Leader: God's kingdom is an everlasting kingdom,
People: AND GOD'S DOMINION IS FROM GENERATION TO
          GENERATION.

— Adapted from Daniel 4:3

God is the author of life,
the creator of love,
the designer of family,
the origin of all things beautiful and good,
the source of joy,
and the object of hope.
Come, let us worship the Lord our God.

INVOCATIONS

God of the universe, we honor you as the creator of all things great and small, beautiful and bright. We see your handiwork above us, around us, below us, and within us. Help us to honor and preserve everything you have made, and to see the throbbing of your life in all that surrounds us.

Speak to us, Lord.
Speak to us through the earthquake.
Speak to us through the wind.
Speak to us through the fire.
Speak to us through the Word and Sacrament.
Speak to us through the still, small voice which whispers in the stillness of the night.

We come to you, O God,
as the Lord of happy surprises,
author of both the ordinary and the miraculous,
who is eager to answer our prayers in amazing ways,
who rewards our faith with even more than we anticipated.
Pour out your Spirit upon us, we pray,
and surprise us even in this hour.

This is God's house.
This is God's day.
This is God's world.
Let us worship the Lord our God.

We have come to this place
to celebrate your good gifts,
to enjoy each other's company as people of God,
to share in a worship experience with our families,
and to bask in your love.
Stand among us and bless us, we pray,
and help us to celebrate with joy.

We honor you as Creator of the universe.
We love you as Savior of our souls.
We serve you as Lord of our lives.
We fear you as judge of the nations.
We praise you as our hope for this life and the next.

Lord, open our ears,
that we may be tuned in to your Spirit.
Lord, open our eyes,
that we may see your majesty all around us.
Lord, open our minds,
that we may understand your will for us.
Lord, loosen our tongues,
that we may worship with enthusiasm and joy.

PRAYERS OF CONFESSION

PRAYER OF CONFESSION

Leader: If we have despoiled the world you have made, polluting its streams and hills,

People: FORGIVE US, CREATOR GOD.

Leader: If we have despoiled the bodies and minds you have given us, though neglect or misuse,

People: FORGIVE US, CREATOR GOD.

Leader: If we have resisted your attempts to restore us and have closed our ears to your invitation,

People: FORGIVE US, SAVIOR GOD.

Leader: If we have failed to imitate your compassion for the poor and your concern for the oppressed,

People: FORGIVE US, SAVIOR GOD.

Leader: If we have steeled our wills against your promptings and sealed our ears to your whispers,

People: FORGIVE US, SPIRIT GOD.

Leader: If we have neglected to pray and to cultivate the inner strength of the soul,

People: FORGIVE US, SPIRIT GOD.

WORDS OF ASSURANCE

God does not leave us alone in our resolve to be faithful. God has given us a living example through the person of Jesus Christ, and God shares with us the empowering presence of the Holy Spirit.

PRAYER OF CONFESSION

God of creation, who looked upon all things and declared them to be good, we as a family of humankind have twisted and destroyed your gifts.

You gave us a garden, and we made it a wasteland.

You gave a rainbow of peoples, and we have introduced prejudice and discrimination.

You gave air, water, and beautiful hillsides, and we have polluted and defaced them.

You gave marriage, and we created infidelity.

You gave minds, and we have harmed them with chemicals.

Forgive us, O Creator, for our misuse of your gifts and your powers, and help us to become better caretakers of what we have and what we are.

WORDS OF ASSURANCE

Of this we can be certain and thankful: that the God who is our Creator is also our Savior; that the God who shares his gifts of abundance also shares his gifts of mercy and grace.

PRAYER OF CONFESSION

O Divine Creator, the heavens proclaim your glory and the earth displays your handiwork. Yet we have sometimes closed our eyes to the beauty of your created world and have allowed the noises of our busy existence to blot out the symphonies of your creation. Even when we have admired the beauty around us, we have neglected to give you the praise. Forgive us for our refusal to be still and know that you are God, and for our failures to see the hand of deity in the things we accept as commonplace.

WORDS OF ASSURANCE

The beauty and marvel of the created world is exceeded only by the beauty and marvel of God's healing grace. The rich provisions he has made for our physical welfare is excelled only by the provisions he has made for our eternal souls.

PRAYER OF CONFESSION

O Creator God, we are ashamed of what we have done to the products of your loving and intelligent power.
What you have created we have misused and polluted.
What you have declared good we have exploited and demeaned.
What you have made for the benefit of humankind we have twisted into instruments of suppression.
What you intended for our comfort we have transformed into objects of greed.

WORDS OF ASSURANCE

For the creation waits with eager longing for the revealing of the children of God ... in hope that the creation itself will be set free from its bondage to decay and will obtain the freedom of the glory of the children of God.

— Romans 8:19, 21

GENERAL PRAYERS

PRAYER OF INTERCESSION
(For the earth God has given us)

Creator God, we pray that we may become better stewards of the earth you have given us—or more accurately, the earth you have loaned to us for safekeeping. May the generations after us receive the legacy of a world fit to live in.

Deliver us, O God, from the greed that would deface or pollute the earth for short-term profit.

Deliver us, O God, from the negligence that would destroy in a few hours the life that has taken years to mature.

Deliver us, O God, from the injustice that would allow the rich and powerful to deprive the poor and powerless of their fair share of the goods that were intended for all.

Deliver us, O God, from the blindness which sees no connection between your created Word, your written Word, and your incarnate Word.

PRAYER OF PETITION
(For an expanded view of love)

Expand our understanding, Lord, of what it means to love, and give us a new knowledge of what it means to care.

Help us to love you by caring for the earth—the earth you molded with so much power and care, and the creatures in which you breathed so much life, calling them good.

Help us to love our neighbors here and around the world by keeping clean the air they breathe, the water they drink, and the food they eat.

Help us to love our children and our grandchildren by leaving a legacy of towering mountains, of fertile plains, of green rain forests, of sparkling streams, of chirping birds, and of prosperous animals of all kinds.

PRAYER OF PETITION
(That we may see beauty in our world)

Creator God, who surveyed all that you had made and declared it to be good, give us the ears, eyes, and hearts to appreciate the world you have given us.

Forbid that we should walk through your world without hearing the songs of the birds, without smelling the flowers along the way, without seeing the glory of the trees, without marveling at the beauty of the hills.

May we not become so numbed by the commercialism of radio and television that we take little notice of the sunset. May we not be so busy with our work that we fail to appreciate the sunshine. May we not be so preoccupied with the things that money can buy that we neglect the riches of experiences which are free.

Give us also a sense of respect for the planet you have given us. May we not burn its forests through carelessness, nor litter its roadsides and beaches with garbage, nor in any way upset the delicate balance of nature. May we respect it for what it is — the work of your own hands.

PRAYER OF PRAISE
(For the things we take for granted)

Hear our prayer of thanksgiving and praise for those aspects of our lives that we often take for granted:

—For the quiet and perfect functioning of our bodies, with their dozens of complete systems, each working in harmony with each other.
—For the orderly progression of day and night, summer and winter, seedtime and harvest.
—For the intricate beauty of butterfly wings, for the awesome grandeur of mountains, for the everyday verdancy of trees and flowers.
—For the sunshine that brings warmth and light, and for the storm clouds that bring life-giving rain.
—For the abundant daily provisions of food and drink, which we simply assume will always be available.

PRAYER OF INTERCESSION
(For ourselves, in our many roles)

As those who live daily with members of our family, we ask for patience and understanding.

As those who are citizens of a world which is constantly at risk, we pray for an attitude of caring and a desire to preserve.

As those who go to work daily, we ask for physical strength and mental sharpness.

As those who are retired, we ask for meaningful activities and for the ability to accomplish them.

As those who seek pleasure and entertainment, we pray for the happiness that produces joy.

As those who are children of God, we ask for lives that are honorable and for ambitions that are responsible.

Care of Creation

OFFERTORY SENTENCES

The earth is the Lord's and all that is in it, the world, and those who live in it.

—Psalm 24:1

For every wild animal of the forest is mine, the cattle on a thousand hills. I know all the birds of the air, and all that moves in the field is mine.... for the world and all that is in it is mine.

—Psalm 50:10,11,12b

Beware lest you say in your heart, "My power and the might of my hand have gotten me this wealth." You shall remember the Lord your God, for it is he who gives you power to get wealth.

—Deuteronomy 8:17-18a

Every good endowment and every perfect gift is from above, coming down from the Father of lights.

—James 1:17

God has given us a world of beauty.
God has given us a world of fertility.
God has given us a world of plenty.
Let us be thankful for it.
Let us preserve it as a sacred trust.
Let us share its bounty with all.
Let us live peacefully together.

God has placed us on earth, not only to be users, but also to be keepers, sharers, and preservers. Let us fulfill God's purpose, not only in this hour but also in our daily lives.

OFFERTORY PRAYERS

As you multiplied the loaves and the bread offered by a small boy of Galilee, so we ask that you will multiply these humble gifts. Invest them in lives which in turn will have an impact on others, resulting in an ever-widening circle of goodness.

Help us, Lord, to be good caretakers of all things—of the money we make, of the time we spend, of the air we breathe, of the flowers we admire, of the earth we walk on, of the streams we splash in—for you have created them all, and they are good.

Not only do we give these gifts for the relief of those who are in poverty, but we pledge to preserve our world and its resources for the good of all. Hear our solemn vow to benefit others not only by sharing, but also by preserving; not only by giving, but also by saving.

Leader: In gratitude for the created world of beauty and plenty,
People: WE GIVE THESE OFFERINGS.
Leader: In gratitude for the new life received in Jesus Christ,
People: WE PRESENT THESE GIFTS.
Leader: In gratitude for the health and strength of each new day,
People: WE OFFER THESE SACRIFICES.

Help us, Lord of the universe and all that is in it, always to be conscious of the fact that we are interdependent creatures — dependent on you and dependent on each other. Help us to be humble in our successes, thankful in prosperity, generous in our sharing, and responsible in the care of our world.

BENEDICTIONS

As you walk from this place,
pause to smell the flowers along the way,
admire God's handiwork all around you,
and live in peace with all of God's creation.

May God bless you
as you respect and protect the earth as a sacred trust
and as a legacy for every generation,
until the new heaven and the new earth have fully come.

Walk in peace with God.
Walk in peace with your neighbor.
Walk in peace with the earth.

In the thunderstorms,
   remember that your life is built upon a solid rock.
In the sunshine,
   pause to enjoy the flowers along the way.
And in the clear starlit nights,
   look upward to experience the majesty of your Creator.

Love the Lord your God.
Love your fellow human beings, made in God's image.
Love all the creatures God has created.

Go forth into the world with joy.
Celebrate the power of God within you.
Hold tightly to that which is good.
Uphold and encourage those around you,
and be at peace with yourself.

Go back into the world—
your world and God's world—
and be guides along the way,
bearers of truth,
sources of life,
and preservers of beauty.

Go forth and live in peace.
Treat your brothers and sisters with honor.
See all creation as a sacred trust.
Walk humbly with your God.

As children of the eternal Father,
live in loving obedience.
As children of the eternal Creator,
live in loving care of all that has been created.
As children of the eternal Spirit,
live in harmony with all that is holy and good.